What peo

T0167498

The Naked Rabbi

Do you want to know what it's really like to be a Rabbi? Then you've got to read this book. It's not an orthodox account but then the author isn't an orthodox man. But it is funny where it should be and moving where it should be, and intellectually stimulating throughout.

Daniel Finkelstein, Associate Editor, *The Times*

Not only is this a fascinating "behind the curtain" look at the day-to-day life of a rabbi, it is one that will resonate with all of us who seek to minister to a religious congregation - its joys, its pains, its challenges. It skewers the lazy idea that the religious professional is other-worldly and only works at weekends. It reminded me what a great privilege it is to be alongside people in their great adventure of faith, however expressed. It's a terrific book.

Giles Fraser, Anglican priest and broadcaster

A fascinating insight into rabbinical life from one of the most prominent holders of this office in the UK, Jonathan Romain is in equal measure informed and entertaining. His position has given him access to key figures engaged with the most significant social and political debates of the past few decades, and his perspective from that of a reform rabbi is truly engaging.

Ruth Gledhill, Online Editor, *The Tablet*

In just one book Jonathan Romain encapsulates the rollercoaster of being a rabbi, or any clergy for that matter. With a depth of warmth and honesty that is so rare, we are taken through the daily delights and difficulties that not only make up the life of a rabbi, but far more importantly, all of our lives. I loved every moment of reading this book, as you will too.

Rabbi Laura Janner-Klausner, Former Senior Rabbi to Reform Judaism

The Naked Rabbi

His Colourful Life, Campaigns and Controversies

The Naked Rabbi

His Colourful Life, Campaigns and Controversies

Jonathan Romain

CHRISTIAN ALTERNATIVE
BOOKS

Winchester, UK
Washington, USA

JOHN HUNT PUBLISHING

First published by Christian Alternative Books, 2022
Christian Alternative Books is an imprint of John Hunt Publishing Ltd.,
No. 3 East St., Alresford, Hampshire SO24 9EE, UK
office@jhpbooks.com
www.johnhuntpublishing.com
www.christian-alternative.com

For distributor details and how to order please visit the 'Ordering' section on our website.

Text copyright: Jonathan Romain 2021

ISBN: 978 1 78904 729 5
978 1 78904 730 1 (ebook)
Library of Congress Control Number: 00000000

A CIP catalogue record for this book is available from the British Library.

Design: Stuart Davies

UK: Printed and bound by CPI Group (UK) Ltd, Croydon, CR0 4YY
Printed in North America by CPI GPS partners

We operate a distinctive and ethical publishing philosophy in
all areas of our business, from our global network of authors to
production and worldwide distribution.

Contents

Previous books by Jonathan Romain

Signs and Wonders (Michael Goulston) 1985 9073720203

The Jews of England (Jewish Chronicle Publications) 1988 0090737204

Faith and Practice: A Guide to Reform Judaism Today (Movement for
Reform Judaism) 1991 0947884084

Tradition and Change (Vallentine Mitchell) 1995 0853033161 (hd)
085303298X (pb) (with Anne Kershen)

Till Faith Us Do Part (HarperCollins) (couples who fall in love across
the religious divide)1996 0006279252

Renewing the Vision (SCM) 1996 0334026571

Your God Shall Be My God (SCM) (on religious conversion in Britain)
2000 0334028094

Reform Judaism and Modernity (SCM) (a survey of Reform theology)
2004 0334029481

God, Doubt and Dawkins (Movement for Reform Judaism) 2008
139780947884

Really Useful Prayers (Movement for Reform Judaism) 2009
9780974884208

Great Reform Lives (Movement for Reform Judaism) 2010
9780947884215

A Passion for Judaism (Movement for Reform Judaism) 2011
9780947884222

Royal Jews (Grenfell Publishing) 2013 9780957698604

Assisted Dying – Rabbinic Responses (Movement for Reform Judaism)
2014 978-0947884246

Terror, Trauma and Tragedy (Movement for Reform Judaism) 2016 978-
0947884253 (with David Mitchell)

Rabbi, I Have a Problem (Jewish Chronicle) 2017 978-1-870216-15-9 with
Naftali Brawer

Confessions of a Rabbi (Biteback Publishing) 2017 978-1-78590-189-8

Inclusive Judaism: The Changing Face of an Ancient Faith (Jessica
Kingsley Publishers) 2020 978-1-78592-544-3

For the Tinxlet (aka Ruben)

Chapter 1

Once Upon a Rabbi

Dad was wrong

Thank goodness I did not listen to my father. I admired him in many ways, and often did follow his advice, but in warning me about becoming a rabbi – wow, did he get wrong! He reckoned that I would be condemning myself to live in an ivory tower, divorced from reality and cut off from the flow of everyday life. Perhaps he was thinking of some of the rabbis of his youth whom he saw leading prayers in a foreign language on the Sabbath and then closeted away in their study the rest of the time: invisible six days a week and incomprehensible on the seventh.

The reality has been very different: modern rabbis are totally immersed in the joys and stresses of the world, with everything in between the two massive traumas we each face, birth and death. So, yes, I was trained to understand liturgy and to delve into textual analysis, but I spend vastly more of my time helping individuals with depression or sitting with those whose partner has just run off. Dealing with addiction, domestic violence and sexual problems are also part of the job spec. Not that it is a daily task sheet of woes: new births, young love, social action, and fun communal projects are common too. As for studying all day, there is the story of the rabbi who was asked what he intended doing now that he had just retired. "There'll be time for a book," he replied. "What will you write about?" they said. "No," he responded, "not write a book, read one!" Rabbinic life is certainly full-on, to the extent that for most of the last forty years I have never been to bed the same day that I got up. That is not a complaint, just a description.

But what kicked it all off? One of the most frequent questions, I am asked by non-Jews is why I decided to become a rabbi in the first place. It comes whenever talking to schoolchildren or addressing interfaith gatherings. My heart sinks every time this arises, as I know I am going to disappoint them. They are expecting an inspirational answer, be it sensing a divine voice that called me, ideally whilst meditating on a mountain-top, or maybe when trudging through a refugee camp (and in both cases, with an orchestra in the background, playing drumrolls and the clash of cymbals). The truth is much more mundane. There was no earth-moving moment, but a gradual process. I had a grandfather who was fairly observant and instilled a love of Jewish tradition within me. I had three superb teachers at Religion School who nurtured my interest in Jewish values. Perhaps it is significant that I cannot remember what they said, but focus more on who they were, and wanted to emulate them in some way. It is all about role models, and although erudite sermons and a wonderful singing voice can help, it is personality that counts. Jewish audiences, incidentally, take a different view and reckon I come from a long line of rabbis and simply went into the family business. Also untrue.

Now that I am the one teaching others, I can only hope that they will think of me the same way that I thought of Gordon Smith, Sidney Fenton and Abe Simons when I was between 11 and 13 years old. My synagogue also had a succession of rabbis who were fascinating characters and so diverse in their styles – intellectual Michael Goulston, informal Lionel Blue and inspirational Adi Assabi. They highlighted what different types of rabbis one could be. But before I get too misty-eyed, I should also recall all those in my class at the Religion School who did not rate them in the same way. So how much is it nature and how much nurture? I also wonder about habit. Clearly I was the product of a positive Jewish home life and good experiences via my synagogue. But what if I had been born into a staunch Anglican or Catholic family, and then attended a vibrant local Church. Might I now be Reverend Romain or Father Romain, rather than Rabbi Romain? Part of me thinks I am so at home in Judaism, that having a different set of beliefs and rituals is impossible to contemplate, but if I was conditioned that way, then maybe this book would be entitled *The Naked Priest* (or even *The Naked Bishop!*).

Even if I cannot remember the actual moment of conception, the idea of being a rabbi was born, and as I grew, it grew too. I suspect that in my teenage years, I had a naive image of what it involved, especially as it was about then that I read James Joyce's *Portrait of an Artist as a Young Man*, and the infamous Father Dolan. I envisaged myself thundering down hellfire and brimstone from the pulpit to my quivering flock. It came as a shock when I realised that we do not have hellfire and brimstone in Jewish theology, but I overcame the setback and persevered with my career path. I also came to realise that sermons form only ten minutes in a much longer day, and only occur once a week anyway. The image of a pastor, spreading comfort and joy, began to take over. Later other images would arise: moral warrior, lonely man of faith, campaigner for important causes, friend to the friendless, communal galvaniser, broadcaster and scribbler. All have their role, and their limits... not to mention their pitfalls. It is what makes a rabbi's life so enjoyable: no day is ever the same, and each day varies: it might start doing a school Assembly, then a hospital visit, followed by a broadcast on the BBC, nipping off to see a congregant in their home and then back to mine to write an article, before doing a funeral. If I say it is hard work, I also have to say it is great fun, immersed in people's lives and sometimes being able to make a difference to them. So to summarise this extremely long answer as to why I became a rabbi, it is a combination of something I thought I would enjoy doing with my life, and that might be useful to others. So, no booming voice from heaven, nor a rose-petal moment of transcendence, but an earthy mix of the selfish and the altruistic.

Putting me off

Still, I was nearly derailed before I had even started. In my late teens, whenever I was visiting a different synagogue I would chat to the rabbi after the service and ask their advice as to what steps to take in preparation. It was very disconcerting to be told by several of them: "Don't do it." On pressing them as to why, they replied that it was a tough job, long hours and little appreciation. I was rather taken aback. I wondered if it was reflection on them not being up to the job and suffering as a result. But I also asked myself if they had sensed something in me that meant I was not suitable. With the uninformed confidence of youth, I decided I would not give in to such negativity and went ahead anyway.

It is not easy becoming a rabbi. Parents can just go ahead and have a baby without any training or giving anyone notice. For a rabbi it takes eight years before we are unleashed on the world. The rabbinic institution, Leo Baeck College, where I went, demands you have a university degree before entry. It can be in any subject, however disconnected to Jewish life, with the idea being that you have reached a certain educational attainment. With so many congregants now going to university, and especially within British Jewry, it is felt important to be on the same level as them. In previous decades, when rabbis were steeped in Jewish knowledge, but little else, their flock sometimes found it hard to respect those with such inferior experience of wider society or current affairs. Many of my fellow students therefore had degrees in law, philosophy or sociology.

I was unusual in that I had followed a narrower course, and had gained a BA in Jewish History and Hebrew Literature. This was due to impatience on my part: having known for so long that I wanted to end up as a rabbi, and having done Common Entrance to get to the next stage of O Levels (today's GCSE) and then taken them to get to A Levels, and passed them in order to reach university, I was keen to start my Jewish studies as soon as possible. Of course, there were also those who either did not decide to enter the rabbinate till after university, or who went into another career first and only switched after several years of doing something else. In fact, my father (still nervous about my direction, although not actually opposed to it) suggested I study law instead, so that I would have other options to fall back on in case I decided the rabbinate was not for me after all. He had a point: many a minister, Jewish or Christians, has found their faith has waned, be it from their own change of heart or under the brutal assault of congregational life, and then what are they qualified to do? I was not offended in his lack of faith in my faith and did initially apply for a law degree, but my impatience rebelled against his common sense, I changed tack and off I went to the Hebrew Department of University College, London.

However, there was another major decision to be made. What sort of rabbi would I be? An Orthodox one, following the dictates of Jewish law, which had been handed down since the time of Moses at Mount Sinai and which adhered to rules that had preserved the faith and could not be changed? Or a Reform one, marrying tradition and change, and believing in Progressive Revelation: that it was not a one-off in the past, but that each generation had to interpret the will of God in its own time and for its own circumstances? To complicate matters more, if I stayed within Orthodoxy, there would be another dilemma as I was the product of a mixed-marriage: my father was Sephardi (the Spanish and Portuguese tradition). His family had been in England since 1781, having come originally from Spain, later crossed to Morocco, gone over to Gibraltar and then to England. (It was via a prestigious means of transport: on HMS Victory and captained by Horatio Nelson – who had taken food and munitions to relieve the siege of Gibraltar and, returning with an empty ship, brought back civilians who wished to escape the bombardment.) My mother was Ashkenazi (the Central and East European tradition) with family roots in Russia, moving to

Poland, settling in Germany and then coming here in 1939 via the kindertransport. To most outsiders, their Judaism is exactly the same, but to insiders there are key distinctions that meant the two groups had often looked askance at each other in the past. After the Second World War, Jews were only too grateful to be alive and so, whereas such unions had been discouraged in previous times, my parents had little difficulty going ahead. I had attended services at both communities and have always considered myself fortunate to have had experience of all three Jewish worlds.

It was the third world, of Reform Judaism, that posed the real challenge for me. Emotionally, I was still very attached to Orthodoxy and the synagogue to which I went with my grandfather and which I continued to attend long after he died. Intellectually, I felt more at home with Reform and the freedom it gave to adapt to new social realities. I also felt I would be more able to relate to congregants as a Reform rabbi, less constrained by regulations that would impede either interacting with them or helping them. For instance, as an Orthodox rabbi, I would not be able to ring a congregant on the Sabbath if their partner had died, or eat at their home if they did not keep strictly kosher. There are ways round this, but they are symptomatic of the barriers to modernity that I knew would become more and more irksome. Even more problematic were the issues that affected people's lives, be it intermarriage or being gay, and where the attitude of "Thou shalt not" was so Canute-like that not only would my rabbinic feet get wet, but my whole ministry would be in danger of drowning. For a while, I hovered and kept a foot in both camps, but in the end I knew there was only one way forward.

My dilemma was not limited to me, but is a tug of faith felt by many Jews: follow emotions or intellect, head or heart? There is nostalgia for "the old ways" and yet attachment to a lifestyle that is incompatible with it. It is epitomised by the popularity of the play, later film, *Fiddler on the Roof*. Jews have flocked to it, hum its tunes and often refer in conversation to its central character, Tevye the Milkman. Yet they would not want to live in the same religious milieu that he did. Tradition is great to wax lyrical about, but not necessarily fit for purpose in today's world. This hesitation helps explain one of the great mysteries in British Jewry today: why the majority of Jews are Reform in their thinking and practice, yet still belong to an Orthodox synagogue. It is even more surprising when they complain about it being irrelevant to their needs, or about its discriminatory attitude to women. So why do they not simply cross the road and join a Reform synagogue?

After almost two hundred years of Reform Judaism in Britain, a steady growth in its communities and the fact that none of its synagogues has been struck by lightning as a sign of God's displeasure, the crossover has been a trickle, not the avalanche one would have expected. But as Tevye sang, it's the pull of tradition, along with the nagging feeling of guilt at having abandoned it, along with a (to my mind) false sense that it was more authentic than is modern Judaism. So they pay their annual subscription to a synagogue whose values they do not endorse. It is not a modern phenomenon, and is ingrained in the Jewish psyche: that every generation is less pious than the previous one and is always looking over its shoulder at the glories of the past. Perhaps it is endemic to religious groups at large, but within Judaism it has often proved a break to progress, feeling unable to make changes. This is despite the fact that many previous generations did enact major reforms when the needs of the time dictated. If Moses came back to life today, he would not only find today's Judaism unrecognisable, but would have felt equally bewildered by it in the first century or the tenth. Unfortunately, the value of modesty – that we are dwarfs compared to the giants of the past, be it a Maimonides or St Augustine – has led to a sense of religious castration that has seen change as the work of the devil (should he exist, which I doubt).

Once you have obtained your university degree, another five years lies ahead at Leo Baeck College. What a curious place! It is named after the iconic rabbi, Leo Baeck, who was the leader of German Jewry during the Nazi years before the Second World War. He already had an international stature though his great learning, which then grew even more because of the dignified way he dealt with the looming tragedy and tried to protect his community as much as he could. When he escorted a group of children to safety in England before the outbreak of the war, rather than remain here, he insisted on returning to Germany to stay with his flock. When he was taken to Theresienstadt concentration camp, he conducted nightly lectures on Jewish history and philosophy so as to boost the morale of the others incarcerated there and to remind them of the higher purpose they had, which the Nazis were so keen to deny. He survived the war and settled in England, passing away only a few weeks after the College opened in 1956 with the task of training a new generation of rabbis and to replace the rabbinic colleges destroyed in Europe.

One of its curiosities is that it trains rabbis for both Reform Judaism and the Liberal Judaism, even though the two movements are completely separate and, as often happens between similar groups fighting over the same religious territory, are keen to maintain their differences. Frankly, if a Martian was to arrive on earth, he would be hard-pressed to distinguish between them. Both adhere to a modern approach to Jewish life, mixing the best teachings of the past with the insights of today. Their services and rituals are virtually the same, they both see women as fully equal, they welcome mixed-faith couples, gays and transgenders into their communities, and they are engaged in causes such as climate change and social action. If the puzzled Martian were to ask why they are separate organisations that mirror each other, and with their own staff who duplicate each other's work, the only answer would be an emotional one: "Tradition!"

There have been many attempts to bring together the two groups, as the differences they once had when they were founded – the Reform in 1840, and the Liberals in 1902 – have long been erased. The talks have foundered primarily because each is precious of its own identity. It is not that far away from the Monty Python's joke in *The Life of Brian* about the rivalry between The Judean People's Front, the People's Front Of Judea, and the Judean People's Popular Front. The Church has similar splinter groups, too, with small groups dividing over miniscule issues. Whether it be religion, politics or the family, we often fall out much more fiercely with those closest to us, and to the mirth of those watching on. The unnecessary divide between the Reform and Liberals is highlighted by the fact that rabbis for both groups train at the Leo Baeck College and take exactly the same courses. In fact, many graduates subsequently switch between the movements in later life, going wherever a pulpit is available and adapting with such remarkable ease that, one day, common sense will prevail and the two will "merge", "unite", "federate", or whatever term allows them to feel they have not jettisoned their principles.

Female rabbis

Another curiosity was that I arrived as the College was opening up to female rabbis. The very first one, Jackie Tabick, had just been ordained as I arrived, and my time there saw several more emerge. Looking back, it is both amusing and sad to recall the battles they had to fight to be accepted, whether by some of the male colleagues or in the congregations they went on to serve. Getting into the College was slightly easier. Whereas the Church went through painful theological convulsions over whether it was possible for women to be priests, in Judaism there was an accidental, but ultimately much more practical sequence of events. It was also helped by the fact that rabbi means teacher and is similar to gaining a PhD in Jewish studies, and without any of the sacramental roles that being a priest has within Christianity. Leo Baeck College – whose stated purpose was "the training of rabbis and teachers" – decided that there was nothing wrong with educating women and imparting Jewish knowledge. At the end of the course, there seemed to be no reason why women should not sit the exam, and once they passed, they became rabbis. So simple!

The next step, being employed, was more challenging. Unlike the Church, where new ordinands were usually sent by their bishop to a particular congregation, with us it is an open-market situation: a rabbi looks for a job, a congregation seeks a rabbi, and if the two like the look of each other, they sign a contract. Many baulked at hiring a female rabbi, fearing that lightning might strike the building on her arrival, or, even worse, the membership would rebel and go elsewhere. In the event, neither happened. At first, people's views were determined by their eyes – "look, someone in the pulpit wearing a skirt!" – but eventually their ears took over, and either she was inspiring or dull, friendly or difficult, and they judged female rabbis in the same way as male ones. Now, with at least 50% of all Reform rabbis being female, the battle is over, even though individuals can still come across pockets of prejudice.

A further curiosity of Leo Baeck College was that when I went there, I was a rarity among students, being one of the handful of home-born ones. Most were from disparate parts of Europe, as well as North or South America, and intended returning there on graduating. This was because the birthplace and beating heart of Reform Judaism – Germany – had now been destroyed, and so the College set out to continue its work and serve a worldwide constituency. This included the United States, where Reform Judaism had become the largest Jewish denomination with its own institutions, but many rabbinic students preferred the British approach to Jewish studies. On the one hand, it was very good for me personally to have so many fellow students from such diverse backgrounds and to learn about their communities' different ways, views and needs. On the other hand, it meant that when I did graduate and emerge into the rabbinate, I had very few contemporary colleagues. There were many other Reform rabbis older than me, but few in my own peer group save a female rabbi in the year below me. I decided that the best course was to marry her – although it was not a purely utilitarian decision – and we had the distinction of being the first two rabbis in the world to marry. In fact, our wedding was sufficiently newsworthy to merit a photograph in *The Times*. Today, we have been joined by several other rabbinic couples.

"What is like being married to a rabbi?" I get asked from time to time. I can only tell them the truth: that I do not know what it is like not being married to a rabbi. The other common question that comes my way is whether our children have become rabbis. When I say that none of them has done so, the person always looks crestfallen, as if they had already prepared a follow-up remark – "Oh, how lovely" – and now cannot use it. I do point out, though, that I never followed in my father's profession, so why should my children follow mine? The person tends to nod politely and amble away, while I am left to feel that I have disappointed them greatly. This highlights the fact that rabbis are not monks. Frankly, if that was a pre-condition for the job, I would never have applied. It is one of the questions that I get asked by children when I am a guest speaker at local schools during their RE class, especially if a Catholic priest had been talking to them the previous week. Fortunately for me (and I am sure most of my colleagues) celibacy is not part of Judaism. It is not even regarded as an ideal for those that can manage it, as St Paul suggested. On the contrary, it is seen as a denial of one of God's gifts and spurning what God has provided for us. There is even a rabbinic legend that when you go to heaven, knock on the gates and request permission to enter, one of the questions you will be asked is: "Did you enjoy all the benefits of the world and make the most of them?" Obviously, our enjoyment should not be at the expense of others, but neither is there anything wrong with having pleasures which are honestly gained, be it a good home, food, wine, or sex. There is no Jewish merit in poverty, which is why we should strive to avoid it both for ourselves and for anyone else. Sexual pleasure, as well as good living, stems from the same imperative that drives us to better the condition of those in need or pain. There are also no hang-ups as to what sort of sex one engages in. As far back as the fifth century, the rabbis of the Talmud (the rabbinic commentary on the Bible) declared that a husband and wife could have any type of sex, specifically referring to discussions around anal intercourse and fellatio (Nedarim 20b). There are more reserved opinions, and certainly traditional objections to sex outside marriage, but Jewish thinking has largely taken the attitude that what happens between consenting adults in private is a matter for them alone.

There is also another objection to celibacy. Enormous weight is put on Jewish continuity. The promise to Abraham in Genesis was that God was establishing a relationship not just with him, but with his descendants (e.g., 12.2; 17.7). Later on, the Book of Deuteronomy makes it clear that to be a good Jew is not enough; you also have to pass it on and teach it to your children (6.7). Without descendants, you have not fulfilled a key part of your side of the covenant with God. Of course, the downside is that this can put a sense of failure on those who do not have children for reasons beyond their control. That is an unfortunate byproduct and congregational rabbis today would insist they are no less Jewish and equally valued. One can contribute to communal life and the next generation in other ways apart from producing offspring. For Jews, therefore, monks and nuns may be respected for their sense of devotion, but are seen as serving God in ways that God would not actually want and that we find unnecessarily self-sacrificing.

Back to the Leo Baeck College: virtually all of the teachers were congregational rabbis who came in to lead classes according to their particular expertise. Among them were names who were well known then within British Jewry, but have become even more revered with hindsight. Such is the benefit of death. They included Lionel Blue, Albert Friedlander, Hugo Gryn, Louis Jacobs and John Rayner. As so often with inspirational figures, their legacy lay not just in what they taught, but how they conducted themselves. Like the Religion School teachers of my childhood, they gave me not just knowledge that I could have found elsewhere, but, more importantly, were examples of how to lead my own life, along with the values to which to aspire. Lionel Blue never stuck to his syllabus (Liturgy), but took us on marvellous journeys to places we might not otherwise have explored. Albert Friedlander (Theology) was rarely prepared, but always shared a depth of wisdom that was exceptional. Hugo Gryn taught Practical Rabbinic from the book of his own life and gave us the confidence to go out and do the job. Louis Jacobs had the hardest task, teaching Talmud, and it was astonishing to be able to study with the most influential scholar that British Jewry has produced in 350 years. John Rayner was assigned Rabbinic Codes, but his lasting lesson was inculcating the highest standards of personal integrity and application. The real test for us – and indeed ministers of all faiths – is not just did we imbibe what was on offer, but will we replace them? Will future generations see us in the same awe-struck light as we now see them, and will our names be spoken of in the same influential tones? If not, then we may be good working rabbis and serve our congregations well, but we will have failed to climb as high as they did.

Study was full time for the initial years, with the final two

years being a sort of sandwich course in which one spent
weekends at a small congregation without a rabbi. Generally,
one year it was a Liberal synagogue and the other year a Reform
one, so as to get familiar with both. (The fact that most of us
found no difficulty in serving both types once again highlights
the minimal differences between the two.) It was a chance for us
to gain experience at real live work and for those communities
to have someone lead services, teach at the Religion School and
provide Adult Education. Looking back, it was very much a
case of being thrown in at the deep end of a swimming pool,
without much guidance save the ire or commendation of the
congregation in its feedback report at the end of the year.
Nowadays, for the first of those two years, students are more
often sent to help out in larger ones with a minister in place,
shadowing the incumbent and being guided by him/her as they
go along.

The first congregation to which I was sent was Maidenhead,
then a synagogue which had never had a full-time rabbi owing
to its small size. It was love at first sight, and fairly mutual. At
the end of my twelve months with them, they suggested that
after my final year as a student, I come back as their first rabbi.
Not that my stint had been without some hiccups. One lesson I
learnt was never to accept an offer of a meal from congregants
before a service. Not only is it best not to take a service on a very
full stomach – you need to be alert for your gig, not ready to curl
over and go to sleep – but, on the one occasion it happened, the
hostess was very behind on the cooking and her timing overran
horribly. Even worse, I had no car then and was dependent on
them taking me to the synagogue to lead the prayers. "Don't
worry," the husband reassured me, "you'll be there well in
time." He was right: thirty seconds beforehand. I made another
discovery that evening: I had expected him to come in and stay
for the service, but he saw his responsibility as simply dropping
me off. To his mind, entertaining the student rabbi for supper

counted as his Jewish deed for the week and absolved him from synagogue attendance.

Expulsion?

I was nearly expelled from Leo Baeck College, with my rabbinic career coming to a premature end, although I never knew it till much later. It became known that I had a non-Jewish girlfriend and apparently the staff held a meeting at which it was discussed and my future debated. At that time, 1977, the furore over Jews marrying non-Jews was at its height. Of course, Jews had being doing this for as long as they had been in England (in fact, even earlier, going right back to the Bible with Joseph marrying an Egyptian and Moses' wife being a Midianite priest's daughter). However, the numbers had been relatively small and there had been strong communal taboos against it. This opposition was based on a threefold concern. First, that the non-Jew would lure the Jew away from the faith. Second, that not only would the Jewish person be lost, but so too would be their children and that whole line cut off. Third, the marriage itself would be likely to end in divorce as religious incompatibilities surfaced and tore the couple apart. These objections were reinforced by parents disowning any offspring who married out of the faith, while the couple would be ostracised by the Jewish community as a whole. It was a religious and social stricture that was sufficient to keep the number of intermarriages very low. However, one of the consequences of the Second World War was that the rate began to rise steadily afterwards, with the evacuation of the Jewish community from its heartland in London in the run-up to the Blitz. It led to synagogues being closed, families parted, children not having any Jewish education and a much greater mingling of Jews with the population at large. Increasingly, Jews and non-Jews mixed together, worked together and, inevitably, fell in love with each other.

As the numbers increased, rabbis began to see intermarriage

as a major threat to Jewish life and started to address it much more, with fiery warnings about its dangers.

In the 1960s, for instance, it was not uncommon to hear sermons describing it as "a cancer in the body of Judaism" or "doing Hitler's work for him". It was colourful imagery – though I would also say, highly offensive – and was indicative of how the religious leadership sensed it was losing the battle. In the past they could afford to ignore it, now they felt it needed full frontal attack. That was certainly true of the Orthodox rabbinate, but it was equally an issue within Reform communities, even if the language was much less strident. This was the context in which my rabbinic future was being discussed. I had met Sarah (a nice Jewish name!) when at university and we had both been members of Nightline, the student equivalent of the Samaritans.

It was a strong relationship and continued into my first two years at Leo Baeck. She had a Catholic faith of her own, but was happy to be involved in Jewish life and traditions. We did not have a definite idea of how things would progress – if we would marry, and if so, if she would convert – but were clearly a couple. You can imagine that if it was bad enough for an ordinary Jew to have a non-Jewish partner, for a would-be rabbi it was much worse. (Some of those fulminating rabbis would say: six million times worse!) It was seen as not only bad in itself, but also a terrible example to others. My situation was therefore raised at a meeting of the College staff and various options considered. These ranged from expelling me to asking us to separate or requesting that Sarah indicate if she was going to convert to Judaism. Apparently, Lionel Blue swung the debate by saying that young love and future marriage were very separate, and the staff should bide their time and see how things developed. All this I discovered years later when one of the lecturers, who had by then become a colleague, told me about the discussion. In the event, Lionel's advice proved prescient, as Sarah and I split up a few months later – although not for religious reasons.

Had he seen something of which we were not aware at the time? Or, as someone who had suffered because of his own love life, had he been typically unwilling to judge that of others? Blissfully unaware of the controversy I had unleashed, I continued to enjoy my time at Leo Baeck, although there were those who did leave prematurely. This was because they realised – or the College told them – that it was an unsuitable career choice. In one case, the person lacked any strength of character. Although, in theory, a religious life should be for the pious, in reality it can involve some brutal fights if you wish to institute changes and introduce new policies or practices. Being meek and mild may be good for the soul, but can result in you being trampled underfoot by congregants keen to do what they perceive as God's will (which, curiously, often coincides with their will). As it happens, I had not necessarily intended becoming a communal rabbi and had imagined I might go into academia. This was partly because I loved study and partly because I reckoned I lacked the "milk of human kindness" and would not be up to congregational work. The omens were not improved when one of my teachers wrote on my annual report: "Teaching Jonathan is like walking up a mountain through a cloud." Did that mean I was dense, enigmatic or simply hard going? Anyhow, he survived the experience and emerged unscathed. It was only in my penultimate year, when I was sent to Maidenhead to serve my compulsory sandwich course year as a student rabbi, that I suddenly realised how enriching communal life could be and that I might not be too bad at it. My final year was spent midweek at the College with weekends at Barkingside Liberal Synagogue (now merged with another community, and known as East London and Essex Liberal Synagogue). Despite my preference for Reform services, I slotted into their liturgy easily and realised how much more united us than divided us. It reinforced my puzzlement as to why we were separate movements ever since.

Chapter 2

River Jews

Fishing for members

My appointment at Maidenhead as their first full-time rabbi was made possible by a chance occurrence. The small community there had unexpectedly come into funds when, along with some adjacent properties, they had sold off part of their extremely long back garden to a developer. He had then put them all together to create sufficient land to build a small housing area. If you want a high income, then you do not become a rabbi, but you still need a salary. This is generally higher than that of a vicar because (although it is now changing in the Church), rabbis no longer receive a tied house, as had been the custom for ministers of both faiths. The thinking was that if for any reason you lost your job or retired, you did not also lose the roof over your head. Instead, we climb onto the mortgage ladder and buy our own homes. It means that, like many of our congregants, there are plenty of expenses when starting out, but hopefully gain a home of your own later on. I was rather amused, therefore, at the theological chutzpah of a local church, which had a sign outside proclaiming "The end of the world is nigh" – when I happened to know that they had just taken out a twenty-five-year mortgage on the building. Were they trying to cheat the bank or just hedging their bets?

The new funds acquired by the Synagogue left them with a choice: use it to improve the fairly dilapidated building or to hire a rabbi? It is a dilemma that many small religious groups face – put your money in bricks and mortar, or in a person who can make the congregation grow? The latter may seem attractive, but given that the person might turn out to be a flop and the money go to waste, might not investing in the building be a safer option? The then chairman, Robert Goodman, took the view that, to paraphrase his thinking, a business without a CEO will never increase its turnover, and that applied just as much to a religious business as a commercial one. Still, the new funds were a one-off, not ongoing, so he told me very candidly that the community could afford to pay me for three years and after that, unless their income improved dramatically, they would have to say goodbye to me. I was, he said, an experiment.

As I am still there, forty years on, I reckon it is fair to say it proved successful. A key part lay in his and my belief that there were many other Jewish people in the area who were not members, but could be persuaded to join. This led to a sustained outreach campaign. Step one was to locate those subterranean Jews. This was done by a variety of means, most simply by asking existing members if they knew anyone Jewish in the area – but always with the promise that their tip-offs would be treated as confidential so that there was no embarrassment at people finding out who had "shopped them". Whenever I visited local groups (being the first real live genuine rabbi in the town, I was much in demand as a speaker), such as schools, church groups, scouts and WIs, I would ask the same question and invariably gained more names. Hospital lists were another useful source of information: whenever I was visiting a member who was unwell, I would ask reception if there was anyone else Jewish who might appreciate a chat (this was in the days before data protection laws stopped personal information being given out). Often there was, and, even better, the person was stuck in bed and unable to escape my tender care extolling the delights of membership.

Step two was to send the unsuspecting victims a copy of our newsletter and a welcoming letter designed to show how user-friendly we were. It also emphasised that we were not just a house of prayer, but a community centre, with many social and cultural activities. This was true, but also based on the assumption that the addressees were not particularly religious, otherwise they would have contacted us already, and so we had to appeal to a different side of them. In this respect, rabbis have a great advantage over vicars when chasing their absconding flock: most Jews who are not at all religious, still feel Jewish and identify with the community. If you are a lapsed Christian and do not believe in Jesus, then Church generally has little attraction for you, save in small villages where it is still the social hub. If you are an atheist or agnostic Jew, however, then you may still regard the synagogue as your home – because you eat Jewish, look Jewish, laugh Jewish, worry Jewish, even if you do not believe Jewish. It means there are still ways of getting Jews to join a synagogue even if they never come to pray in it. In fact, a high percentage of those who have served on the Synagogue Council at Maidenhead and spent hours each week helping to run it rarely attend services. Instead, they shun God, but religiously come to social and cultural events.

Step three is to then follow up in person. In the days when everyone had landlines rather than mobiles, it was relatively easy to obtain their number from the local telephone directory. Less predictable was the reaction when I cheerfully announced: "Hello, I'm Jonathan Romain, the rabbi at Maidenhead Synagogue. I thought I'd give you a call as I heard you were Jewish and living in the area." A few times, it was a snarl – they had been discovered and their anonymity had been blown – and the phone was slammed down. The first time that happened, it was upsetting, but subsequent rebuffs washed over me; after all, it was only a voice down the line, not a punch in the face. One person whispered hoarsely: "My wife does not even know I am Jewish, so how the hell did you find out?" Other times, there was a polite "yes, thanks for the call, but I am not interested." Occasionally, it was "Sorry, I am not Jewish." This was usually because my informants had taken a guess based on the person's surname and got it wrong. This applied especially to all the Jacobs to whom I was recommended and who, when they answered in a Welsh accent, I knew what was coming next.

In most cases, though, there was mild interest, either intrigued by the call or chuffed that a rabbi had bothered to ring, which was often a new experience for them. That was the opportunity for me to say that "It just so happens that I am going to be passing by your house next week [subtext: timely coincidence, so why not taken advantage of it, and much easier than you having to go out and meet him at the synagogue], so maybe I can pop in for five minutes [subtext: don't worry, I won't be there for hours] and say hello [subtext: friendly chat, not trying to drag you off to prayers]." In many cases, the offer was accepted and, as any salesman will tell you – and, to come clean, I am a fully paid up religious salesman – getting your foot in the door is half the battle. Thankfully, have a good sense of directions, which is vital when visiting people in rural areas without any street lighting and when the only directions are "past some fields, then down a lane on the left after the post box" (all of which are invisible in the dark). But I always get there on time.

Once I was sitting in their living room, the five minutes became an hour. At that point, two things invariably happened. First, almost all said that they had never had a rabbi visit them – even when they had previously lived in London or another place where they had been members of a local synagogue – and it was nice to chat to a rabbi in their own home, rather than just peer at him in the pulpit. Second, a high percentage said "Actually, we've wanted to speak to a rabbi for a while because we have this issue..." It might be a status issue, concern about burial arrangements or what to do about a black sheep in the family. It was remarkable how many domestic cupboards had a skeleton (or two) in them. The visits showed the value of the rabbi taking the initiative to go to them, rather than waiting for them to approach the rabbi. They also felt much more comfortable, feeling at ease in their own home. Although some visits resulted in a pleasant "Well, it was nice to meet you, but we won't be joining," in other cases I left with their membership form and cheque in my hand (though nowadays it is more likely to be a Direct Debit form as the latter start disappearing from usage). Why had they not done so of their own accord? Some because they had never got round to doing it, some because they did not even realise there was a synagogue in the area, and some because they had had bad experiences in their previous synagogue before moving to the area. In case you are interested, whereas only 50% of the phone calls got me an invitation to come round, once there and able to show the friendly face of the community, around 75% of them joined. In business terms, that is a good hit rate.

Pay-as-you-pray

In case it is not clear (and to explain the reason for me taking away a cheque), Jews join a synagogue by paying an annual subscription. It is like signing up for the RAC or National Trust. This enables members to come along 365 days a year or anything less. It is far more efficient than the Church custom of making an offering during the Collection, which is effectively a pay-as-you-go system, whereas ours is a pay-even-if-you-never-go system. It also makes the treasurer's job much easier, as he can be certain how much his annual income will be each year, while it gains funds from those who do not wish to attend very often but still want to support the synagogue from afar. This can be a surprisingly large group of people who find they either have no time to get to the synagogue, or no inclination to do so, but still believe it should exist and be there for those who do want to take advantage of it. This in turn highlights the fact that synagogues are totally self-supporting. There is no government funding, nor any central Jewish financial support. Synagogues exist only because there are a sufficient number of Jews in the area who are willing to pay the annual subscription. That is why Maidenhead never had a full-time rabbi from when it started in 1940 till when I came along in 1980. They could pay for the upkeep of a small building and the limited salary for a student-rabbi, but nothing more. The reverse is also the case. When large established synagogues lose members because of demographic changes, their income goes down and the subsequent cost-cutting may well result in the rabbi departing, with lay leaders taking the services and fulfilling other functions.

It was a vital part of the membership drive, therefore, not only to gain members, but to keep them. Bearing in mind that they did not especially want to join in the first place, but had only done so as a result of me contacting them out of the blue and then sitting in their front living room until they signed up, it meant making sure of two things. First, that there were plenty of activities on offer that would be of interest to them: not just services, but a host of social, cultural, educational, welfare and sporting events. These included book circle, table tennis club, bridge group, poetry evenings and cricket team, as well as one-off speakers or cookery evenings. Intriguingly, we found that adult education classes attracted more than services: people wanted to learn Hebrew, but rarely came to use it; they wanted to study Jewish history, but not spend time with God. It was no accident that when we had the lovely problem of first rebuilding the synagogue to accommodate the greater numbers, then moving to a considerably larger venue, and recently having to enlarge it even further, the space designed for social events was much bigger than the prayer hall. The second key aspect of retaining members was making them feel welcome when they did come. Nobody was allowed to stand alone and feel like a wallflower (wallflowers may not move much when they first come, but after standing around and being ignored, they never appear again). People were greeted, and introduced to others. What mattered was not how often they came, but that, when they did come, they really enjoyed the experience.

There are many colleagues who do not see it as their job to bring in new people – that is the task of the membership committee – or who find it embarrassing knocking on the doors of strangers. Fair enough, and they have skillsets in other areas that I lack. But for me, growing the membership was much more than a financial exercise or ensuring the synagogue's continuity. I saw it as religious work, because I passionately believe in keeping Jews Jewish, and without being part of a synagogue, the link weakens and eventually disappears. It is not enough to have a Jewish feel or Jewish friends; one needs to have the umbilical cord of being connected to communal life. Without it, like a spaceman who loses his attachment to the spaceship, you drift off and are lost forever. But I have another motive: that I genuinely believe that belonging to the community will enrich their lives and that they personally will benefit from it. This could be making new friends, or deepening their Jewish knowledge, or feeling part of something worthwhile, or having a safe space, or gaining a sense of spirituality, or finding a sympathetic ear for various problems, or developing their leadership skills, or valuing a link with tradition. I derive enormous pleasure from seeing someone who told me forcefully that they have not been to synagogue for several years and did not intend changing, now become a stalwart of the photography group, help with lunches for the homeless or join the Council – both because they are doing great things for the community and because I know they have gained from it themselves. We have long ceased to cover just Maidenhead, for our members come from both sides of the river and across several counties as the Thames wends its way upstream from Windsor to us, then onto Marlow, Henley, Reading and Oxford, as well as many other towns and villages further afield.

Although I was not bothered at being told that I only had three years at Maidenhead "before the money ran out", certain it would prove wrong, I did have a more immediate issue that faces many a minister starting his career: asserting my authority. There are, of course, different styles of religious leadership. Some prefer to lead from the back, being supportive of others and seeing their role as facilitators (which can be very helpful, or can end up with them being the communal dogsbody and treated as a wimp). Others lead from the front and see it as their duty to take the congregation in a certain direction (which can lead to enormous progress, or can result in them being dictatorial and resented). Others take their authority from the written text and will quote their scriptures (which can lessen personal foibles, or can become stultifying, always locked in the past, as well a the victim of interpretation). Danger lurks everywhere! In my case, I faced a triple hurdle: I was young, I was new, and I was the first full-time rabbi, so the synagogue was used to being led by a group of lay members who were long established and had been revolving positions on the Council for several years.

Banned from Russia

An early test came within my first year when I campaigned over Soviet Jewry. At that time, Jews in the then USSR were discriminated against, being denied access to promotion at work (all of which was under state control) and unable to teach their children about the faith. Yet when they tried to emigrate and go to Israel or other countries, they were refused permission, and became known as "refuseniks". As they could not leave, Jews outside the USSR would visit them, both to show support and to give classes in Jewish knowledge. I had done this as a student rabbi, visiting the country three times. All trips had to be through a tour group, not individual journeys, as all foreigners were closely monitored, but once inside the country, we would skip the official activities and slip off to make home visits. When I applied again, I was denied a visa, because they had realised what I was doing and wished to prevent any further "interference" (as they saw it). My immediate response was to tell the local paper, the *Maidenhead Advertiser*, for another part of the campaign was highlighting the plight of Soviet Jews and trying to pressurise the Soviet authorities to release them. This was in the midst of the Cold War and the paper, delighted to have an international issue, rather than report on local parks being vandalised or prize marrows being grown, put it on the front page. There was a blazing headline: MOSCOW SAYS "NO" TO RABBI'S RUSSIAN TRIP, with a large print quote underneath: "Perhaps it's because I'm a Jew".

One of the leading Council members was horrified, on the grounds that the Synagogue had always kept a low profile, with memories of the days when antisemitism was more common, leading to an attitude of "don't cause a fuss, don't draw attention to ourselves". I understood that, but differed from it: we lived in a different era, and although we should not be pushy, we should not hide our identity either. If churches could have big signs outside their buildings and have items in the paper about their events, so could we. It was also another strategy in my membership drive: to advertise our existence and let Jews, who simply did not realise there was Synagogue locally, know we were here. This applied particularly to the growing numbers who were moving to the area from London, but who had retained their membership of communities there without appreciating there was a more local option. At the next Council meeting, that person reprimanded me and demanded that my public activities cease. I was taken aback, but told Council that I considered it an important part of my rabbinic role and that it would not change. Silence. It was a critical moment as to whom Council would back. Another member sitting round the table said "I think we have to come to terms with that's the way Jonathan is." The chairman moved on to the next item on the agenda and at the following meeting the individual objecting resigned.

Ever since that moment I have virtually always had the full support of both successive Councils and the community as a whole. There have still been the odd occasion when a particular course of action was questioned, and sometimes I have decided that it might be best not to take that route. But, although I have often faced fierce criticism outside the community over various causes I have adopted – be it on mixed-faith marriages, faith schools or assisted dying – I have not had to face fights in my own backyard. This leads me on the Romain theory of the rabbinate (though it is applicable to ministers of other faiths too). I know that I am perceived by some as having taken controversial stances (though to me they are simply a matter of common sense!), yet my position at Maidenhead has always been secure. Other ministers have been much less outspoken, yet have faced challenges within their community, given warnings or even lost their job. Why this discrepancy? My theory is that providing your congregation feels you know them and love them, they will excuse a lot of opinions or actions with which they do not agree. As one member said to me, when explaining why his cousin in Manchester thinks I am atrocious and should be sacked: "I told him, look Jonathan's been to my house, knows me, my wife, knows the children's names and even knows the name of our pet rabbit – who cares if he has some crazy ideas every now and then. He's alright and he's always got time for me." His remark highlights how what counts for congregants is not the quality of your sermons, but the strength of your personal relationships. When visiting other synagogues, I have seen colleagues give sermons that were dire, and whom I am told are regularly uninspiring, but who are clearly loved by congregants. They feel that what he or she lacks in oratory, or in other areas of their ministry, they make up for in warmth and kindness. Congregants will tolerate your lapses, eccentricities or daft views, but not your coldness, indifference or not knowing their names. The latter is a small matter in the scheme of life's problems, but carries enormous weight and is often taken to imply (wrongly) that you do not care about them or that they are irrelevant.

However, it is a very selective memory, good with people and what has happened over the years in their personal lives, but poor on facts relating to other matters. You can always tell a book I have read as the margins are filled with notes in pencil, highlighting key points, as I would otherwise forget them entirely and have to reread the book. This is so chronic that I have been in the position of reading an article in a magazine, found it fascinating, enjoyed lots of information that I did not know and wished I had been able to write something along those lines. I have then turned over the page, reached the end and, to my great surprise, found I had written it myself. I had forgotten both that I had done so and most of the information I had detailed. I suppose it is a form of mind-dump, clearing space in my memory, so that I can move on to the next topic. I know it sounds ridiculous, but it has happened twice.

Another test of my authority that same year was when I had to face down my Senior Warden. The congregation was in possession of two scrolls – which contain the Five Books of Moses and from which we read extracts at Sabbath morning services. They had been loaned to us from a synagogue in the East End of London when Maidenhead had started in 1940 as an evacuee community, with Londoners flocking to the Home Counties to avoid the Blitz. Out of the blue came a letter saying that the synagogue was closing and its assets (including the scrolls, which are expensive items costing several thousand pounds) were being taken over by another community and so could they have them back please. It sent the Council into a panic. Replacing them would be enormously expensive and way beyond our means, but we could not function without having any scrolls. What to do? The Senior Warden had a brainwave.

In a scene that felt like being in the middle of an episode from *The Vicar of Dibley*, he suggested that we say we were very sorry, but we no longer had them in our possession and so could not oblige. A few others round the table seemed impressed. I felt I had to jump in quickly and point out that this was not only theft, but also theft of religious items, one of whose purposes was to remind us of our moral obligations. The Senior Warden glared at me, leaned forward as if about to say something, but then sat back and decided not to argue the point. In the end, we did return the scrolls, having negotiated an extra loan period to give us time to fundraise for new ones. I still wonder what might have happened had he forced a vote and won it. Hiding the scrolls under the floorboards and taking them out for a furtive read each week while someone kept watch at the door was not part of my contract.

Actually, I did not have a contract. For some reason, no one had thought of drawing one up. I did not object as I had a letter of engagement, which I reckoned was sufficient, with the only stipulation being that we could give each other six months notice. Looking back, that was probably short of the legal requirement for an employer-employee relationship. Also, most rabbis preferred a fixed period of service, such as three or five years, to be reviewed at the end of its term, so as to give them some security. However, it seemed to me that if the community objected to me for whatever reason and the relationship soured, there would be no point staying on. Similarly I was happy to have the freedom to say goodbye to them whenever I wanted.

It was only after thirty-eight years at Maidenhead that an on-the-ball Council member said this was an untenable situation, that a formal contract was drawn up. Nothing changed, but it means that I now had the legal protections that, thankfully, I had never needed up to that point. Certainly, many a rabbi has found that even though they were serving the community at large well, a small group within it can take a dislike to them and make their life unpleasant. If that group happens to consist of Council members, then, whatever the views of the congregation at large, it can lead to their dismissal unless they have the protection of a contract and grievance procedures. But neither should incumbents be above criticism or removal if rabbis are poor at their job or behave badly. If you can sack a useless salesman or fire a terrible chef, you should also be able to get rid of a rogue rabbi or an under-performing minister.

The boss (aka God)

As for my supreme boss, one of my most remarkable study sessions was when I asked those present to draw their concept of God. Bearing in mind that Jews do not depict God in any way, this initially produced shocked reactions. When I explained that it was not a heretical attempt to "capture" God on paper, but to express our own personal sense of what God meant to us, everyone did so. To their surprise, they found it a very easy exercise, as they had clearly long held their own private images. For one, it was an eye: God is all-seeing, and knows not only our actions but also our thoughts. Even if we wanted to do so, there is no hiding from God. For another it was a tree: God is nature and the genius behind the complex interdependence of our ecosystem, with each creature contributing to it being sustained and perpetuated. Allied to this was God as sunset or dawn: the regularity which we take for granted, but which is truly amazing. We go to sleep each evening confident that day will follow night, as will autumn arrive after summer, and the cycle of the year continue. Very different was God as a hand. This is the power who intervenes in our affairs, be it publicly in biblical times or in less transparent ways today. For some, the latter are mighty acts such as the collapse of Communism; for others it is the unexpected rescue of individuals who seemed doomed.

Naturally God featured as creator, with a drawing of the

globe, or a law-giver, as in the two Tablets of Stone. But there was also a mobile phone: the God with whom we can relate to on a one-to-one basis. Some depictions were incompatible with those of others: the puppet-master who pre-ordains our lives as we dance to a divine tune does not sit well with the parent who has brought us up but then lets us go our own way. More intriguing was the check-out till supervisor, who waits patiently as we wend our path through various aisles in the supermarket of life, choosing options and rejecting others, but ultimately having to reach the end-point, when what we have is assessed and needs to be paid for. Personally, I liked the word-bubbles drawn above a head. God is the still small voice of conscience, first mentioned by Elijah, but still resonating today. It tells us that we really should not do what we are intending; or that we should do the very act that we want to avoid. Many will find sympathy for the individual who simply drew a giant question mark. It was not so much out of a sense of ignorance, but asking how is it possible to comprehend a force so far beyond human understanding? For them, any one image or word can only be partial, and is too limiting to be of any use. Taken together, the images are all true – even those that contradict each other – and testify to the uniqueness of God, as well as how differently God can seem to each individual, as is also the case for different faiths. Perhaps they also indicate our own uncertainties, for many admitted that different pictures applied at different points of their life, and so much depends on what *we* are going through, not who God is. Hopefully, if God is reading this (so to speak), God is laughing: "Of course they cannot sum me up; only the arrogant or the manipulative claim to know Me fully. Rather than compete with all their claims about Me, it would be better if they concentrated on some of my requests, and getting on with each other is top of the list."

Chapter 3

Hatch (and Beyond)

Bumps and Birth

A vicar's life is sometimes caricatured as surrounding the three crucial moments of "hatch, match and dispatch" (though in a world where divorce is now prevalent, I will add "scratch"). For rabbis, we have the six bs: birth, *brit milah* (circumcision), baby blessings, bar/batmitzvah, betrothal and burial. It might be realistic to add "breakup" to the alliteration, for the time spent dealing with relationships which fail. Each stage can involve a mix of emotions for the families concerned and some delicate pirouetting by the rabbi to help them, maintain his/her own integrity and stay within Jewish tradition.

Rabbis are not usually present at the birth of a child, unless it is their own. In my case, I found it not just a medical experience, but a profoundly religious one. One moment, there was my wife and myself, just the two of us, the next moment we had become three. It is the only time I have felt I was witnessing the occurrence of a miracle. What appeared just to be a bump became a living, breathing, squawking person. We take it for granted, but it is an amazing process. However, although nowadays we are used to everything going smoothly and expect all pregnancies to be successful, that is not the case. The incidence of miscarriages is much higher than imagined, as many couples keep the news to themselves.

But they are still pained by it. However much one is aware that it is nature's way of aborting a foetus that is defective in some way, it still hurts and there can be a sense of failure that one had not been able to do what other couples had achieved. Of course, they do not know if the happy mum and dad whom they pass in the street pushing along a buggy has also experienced a miscarriage previously, but logic is no help for an emotional wound. While some ministers may try to offer the comfort that it is the ineffable will of God, a line that may have worked in previous eras, my suspicion is that today it just makes them hate God. All one can do is be there with them, whether it be their silence, tears, questions or rages. A soft voice and kind eyes is much better than any attempts at theological justification.

The grief is obviously much greater when there is a stillbirth or the child dies within a few days. By then the nursery may have already been painted, baby clothes acquired and a name for the child chosen. Jewish tradition stipulates that a child that dies under thirty days old does not have a standard funeral. Instead, the body is buried in an unmarked spot, no one attends and no mourning rituals take place. This dates back to the time when there was a high infant mortality rate and the parents were encouraged to treat it as if the child had never existed. Rather than be engaged in needless grief, they should look forward to a positive outcome next time. This was seen as an act of kindness, especially as mourning rituals lasted a year and would be burdensome. Today, however, it feels callous. It also ignores the fact that even if the child had only breathed for a short time, the mother had felt it for several months, while the father may have talked to it and patted it. It existed in their minds, and some form of recognition for its loss is needed. In most cases, therefore, a full funeral takes place and a headstone later erected at the grave. What is different is the eulogy: not about the life that was lived, but the life that might have been and the hopes that were dashed. Every funeral is a time of sadness, but the sight of a small coffin, tiny enough to be carried in the arms of the funeral director, is always amongst the most poignant.

Another form of loss is when the couple discover that one of them is infertile. It can follow years of frustration at trying to have a child without any results, and then a sense of failure and inadequacy when the reason is discovered. One father cheerfully told me he was "firing blanks", but most are not able to joke about it. Instead they face the dilemma of whether to adopt a child or seek medical assistance via a donor egg or sperm. I always find this a tricky debate. Morally, I reckon that it is far better to adopt and to give a good home to an existing child who lacks it. However, I totally understand those who wish to have a child that at least "belongs" to one of them. Orthodox rabbis would object to the latter on the grounds that it is a form of adultery, but I think that is being over-technical and does not correspond to reality. More of a problem, to my mind, would be if one partner felt it would be difficult to develop a relationship with the subsequent child, knowing that it was not actually their progeny. Adoption, too, has its pitfalls: how to strike a balance between the child knowing it is adopted (which is always the best course, rather than not knowing and finding out later, be it being sat down at some point and told "the truth" or discovering accidentally), yet feeling secure and loved. One couple I know went overboard on the honesty side, making it a constant theme of the child's life. The result was that when I first went to visit them, the then eight-year-old girl shot out her hand in greeting and said "Hello, nice to meet you, I'm Karen (not her real name) and I'm adopted." She did the same thing whenever she met others for the first time.

Circumcision and baby blessings

Thankfully, most couples are able to have children, and if it is a boy, the question of circumcision immediately arises. Traditionally, the ritual takes place eight days after birth, unless the child has a health or weight issue, in which case it is delayed until he is fully fit. However, whereas once the circumcision was seen as a joyous occasion, fulfilling one of the earliest commands given by God to Abraham and to be passed on to all his descendants (see Genesis 17.10 ff.), now it can sometimes be viewed in a very different light. Words such a "barbaric" and "mutilation" are used in some circles. This is partly because of greater concerns over child protection, which are to be welcomed; partly because of the large number of Muslims in Britain today, who also perform circumcision, albeit up to thirteen years old, and worries that some practitioners are not as skilled as they should be; and partly because of the abhorrence over female genital mutilation (FGM), which is wrongly categorised as akin to male circumcision. It means that rabbis are often put in the position of having to defend circumcision to a sceptical, if not hostile wider public. Inevitably, this negative atmosphere can have an effect on Jewish families. It is not uncommon for a pregnant mother, when asked if she is carrying a boy or a girl, to reply with a knowing look "I'm not sure, but I'm praying for a daughter." The degree of questioning within the Jewish community has also risen due the increase in the number of Jews marrying non-Jews. While the Jewish partner may not be looking forward to the ceremony, they have four thousand years of tradition pushing them along. For the non-Jewish partner, however, it can seem strange, if not outrageous.

In reality, virtually all circumcisions are problem free. Unlike FGM, there is no harm done sexually. There is also no evidence of any psychological damage, for no Jews (including me) have any memory of what happened to them at eight days old. As the dad of four boys, I can also attest that although they gave a yelp at the time, the combination of having a drop of wine (the equivalent for you and me of a bottle of whisky) and then going on the breast for a feed, meant they then slept it off and were fine in the next day or two. I certainly did not worry about the person doing it, as Jewish circumcisers (*mohalim;* plural of *mohel*) are highly trained specialists. On the positive side, there are the health benefits, preventing various diseases of the penis, which is why some non-Jewish men are circumcised in later life for medical reasons. These were certainly very strong advantages in earlier times, and are still a factor today. During a synagogue tour I helped organise to South Africa, we passed giant billboards for the AIDS campaign depicting a woman looking at you suggestively and declaring, "I like it condomised and circumcised." Ultimately, though, it is a religious ceremony, a sign of the covenant. It is often forgotten that although the ceremony happens to the child, the real onus is on the parents. It is they who make the decision and they who make the act of commitment to pass on the Jewish heritage to their child. Of course, this then begs the question of some (but not all): what does it say about them if they decide not to go ahead?

Amid these swirling cross-currents, the rabbi has a multiple role. On one level it is to explain the background and religious significance to couples expecting a child. I never tell them what they have to do, but do tell them that they should decide either way long before the birth. Once he arrives, they will be emotional and sleep-deprived, and in no state to make a decision. I also reassure them that the only *mohalim* we use are practising doctors or surgeons, so they are not only religiously appropriate but medically qualified. I tell those parents concerned about the possible pain to the child, that they now routinely use anaesthetic cream on the penis. If parents are particularly anxious I mention that, instead of holding the ceremony at their home, as is the usual custom, it can be done in the doctor's surgery. Between you and me, it is conducted in exactly the same way as at the home, but it can feel safer and more professional, and perception is everything. Personally, I reckon they are much better off at home, where they feel more at ease and where family can crowd in to support and distract. I appreciate that it seems extraordinary to non-Jewish relatives that a medical operation takes place in the front living room, and that family and friends are invited to look on (hospital operations do not have a viewing gallery!), but that is the tradition. Another tradition is for the baby to take revenge on the *mohel* by peeing on him as he takes off the nappy. When present, my unofficial role is to stand behind the father in case he faints, as occasionally happens. I have learnt that the more macho the person, the more likely they are to wobble. I have had to prop a few up, but the only one I had to catch was an Israeli paratrooper. He was fine facing great danger on active service, but when it came to his little son, down he went. Still, as the circumcision literally takes under ten seconds, dads can often miss it if someone starts chatting to them.

If parents decide not to go ahead, then I usually have to deal as much with the distraught grandparents as with them. In either case, although I personally favour circumcision, I can assuage feelings of anger or guilt by pointing out that the child will be no less Jewish. Circumcision, or the lack of it, does not affect religious status. It is not as if the baby is non-Jewish for the first seven days after birth and then becomes Jewish upon circumcision. He is Jewish the moment he is born, so if the ceremony does not occur, he is simply an uncircumcised Jew. He may feel odd that he is different from most other male Jews in this respect (though they are unlikely to know). Alternatively, he may regret it did not happen at birth if he decides, for medical or religious reasons, to have it done in later life. But his Jewishness is not in question.

Baby blessings have experienced a remarkable change. They were introduced in Reform synagogues as a ceremony for girls to match the initiation for boys, albeit in a very different way, and as an opportunity for a family celebration of the new arrival. The parents bring the child to synagogue, stand before the open ark, each read a short prayer and the girl is welcomed and officially named. Some rabbis do it midweek, or in the parents' house, but I have always encouraged them to do it as part of a Friday evening or Saturday morning service – both to encourage them to see the synagogue as a second home, and to share their joy with the rest of the community. But over the years, more and more parents have opted to have it for boys as well. For those who do not want to have their son circumcised, it is a substitute way of affirming his Jewish identity. For those who do have the circumcision, it is a more relaxed ceremony, less rushed than the eight-day one, and less stressful for them.

Meanwhile a new ritual has been invented for girls, *simchat bat*, literally "rejoicing over the daughter". It is a domestic ceremony, initially attended by the women in the family and female friends, with songs, poems, readings and blessings to greet the new arrival. Now, however, invitations are extended to everyone. It is part of a new wave of religious thinking to cater for the many areas of a woman's life that have tended to be neglected. This has also extended to healing rituals after a miscarriage, or prayers on reaching menopause. It also reflects the arrival of women rabbis who have opened up creative new avenues, which male colleagues never thought of. But the ceremony can be lay-led and is the result of the much greater involvement of women in Jewish decision-making, as well as the greater Jewish education they have, and hence their confidence to develop new rites.

However, a birth can still bring complications over names. One father shocked his relatives by calling his son Christopher – a name with specifically Christian associations and generally not used by Jews. Moreover, he was one of our more observant members, so his choice was even more puzzling. It turned out that his adherence to tradition was what had led him to do it. Most Jews have two names: the one they use in public and the one that is used in synagogue for when they are called up to take some part in the service. The latter is almost always a Hebrew name, and often matches the secular one in some way, such as having a similar sound or initial letter. Sometimes both may coincide, such as being called Daniel or Sarah, which can be used in both domains. Other times, they can be completely separate e.g., a person known as Roger in wider society might be called Reuben in synagogue. Unlike other parents, this particular father chose the Hebrew name first – Chaim – and then wanted an English name that began with "Ch" and ended up with Christopher. Had he thought longer, there would have been other options. The one forename that no Jew has ever used in the last few decades is Adolf, because of its terrible associations with the Holocaust. Historically, however, it was commonly used among Jewish families, including by some leading rabbis.

A different type of problem can occur when someone from an Ashkenazi (Central and East European) background marries someone who is from a Sephardi (Spanish or Mediterranean) background. The former have the tradition of naming a child after someone who has died, so as to maintain their memory; the latter prefer to name after someone who is alive, so as to honour them in their lifetime. Both are lovely customs, but can lead to misunderstandings if, for instance, they have a girl, follow the husband's Sephardi tradition and name their daughter after the Ashkenazi wife's mother (who is very much alive) and she takes umbrage, thinking her son-in-law wants her dead! Other couples can be very inventive to both keep traditions but simultaneously get round them. One of them, for instance, felt they ought to name their child-to-be after a relative called Martha who had died recently, even though they did not care for the name. They were saved by the fact that the baby turned out to be a boy, and so, taking the first two letters of her name, he became Matthew. This highlights the problem that many secular names go out of fashion, and so calling your offspring after someone from a previous generation can seem archaic. But we are helped by the fact that, as a generalisation, many Jews still prefer to opt for biblical names – as they can double up for both one's Jewish and general name – and they tend to fluctuate less in the popularity stakes.

The only time I decide to intervene in this personal minefield is when a couple tell me that they will not chose a name till after the baby is born. I warn them that it almost certainly will not look like a Max or Rachel or Joseph or Emily; instead it will most closely resemble a squashed tomato, and that is probably not a good choice. Conversely, if they already have a name in place, then he or she will neatly slip into it and own it immediately. If they raise their eyebrows at my earthy depiction of their baby, I tell them about the single mother in the community who did wait till after the birth to find a name. None seemed to fit, the days went by and turned into weeks. The legal limit by which time you have to register a child's name, six weeks, began to fast approach. The joy of the new arrival began to be overshadowed by anxiety over what to call him. She chose a name just before going to the Registry Office, nearly risking a fine and exasperating all those whose attempts to make helpful suggestions she rejected.

Bar/batmitzvah

It is a sign of the times that the word "barmitzvah" is sufficiently well known in society at large not to be explained. This may be partly due to television programmes about Jewish life and featuring the time when a thirteen-year-old boy comes of age (in religious terms) and reads from the scrolls in synagogue. Alternatively, it may be due to the fact that his parents now do something that only three or four decades ago was virtually unheard of: invite non-Jewish friends or work colleagues to the ceremony. It was not that they were prevented from doing so before; it was more that they were embarrassed at what the non-Jews might make of such an alien experience, or they reckoned that they simply would not be interested. In reality, they are usually delighted to be invited and fascinated by what happens. The initial nervous few invites have now turned into a regular occurrence and it is rare for me not to be asked if we have spare head coverings for non-Jewish guests. The same applies to a batmitzvah, the ceremony for thirteen-year-old girls which, in Reform and Liberal synagogues, is identical to that of boys. In Orthodox congregations, where women are not able to have the same role as men and sit separately from them, it is done differently.

The willingness to share a quintessential Jewish rite of passage has extended to the children too, most of whom will now invite their friends from school. It would have been unthinkable when I had my barmitzvah: there was a strict separation between my Jewish life and my place in wider society. Never did the two worlds cross. Similarly, I had Jewish friends from the Sunday morning Religion Classes and non-Jewish friends from school, but I never mixed seeing one group with the other. Had I invited any of the latter to my service, who knows what teasing at school might have resulted or what stories would have been told on Monday morning about strange Jewish goings-on? Today it is so different, and I always sneak a look at the friends of the barmitzvah boy/batmitzvah girl as he/she reads from the Hebrew scrolls: invariably their jaws drop. Most would be aghast at having to speak in public, let alone in a foreign language, while they are amazed that their friend can read Hebrew when they do not even know which way to hold the book. To say that he/she walks tall in their eyes is no exaggeration.

The ceremony itself can have a special effect on the actual child. Back in the first century, reaching thirteen signalled a boy was about to reach adulthood and was about to emerge into the world of work. This aspect has long passed, and to a certain extent the milestone lost some of its relevance. Instead, it became about religious adulthood, the ability to read from the scrolls and to count in a quorum for those prayers that traditionally required the presence of ten men. Curiously, it has now gained a different significance. At the very moment when the teenager turns into a monosyllabic hoody, prefers to sit in the shadows rather than be involved in family life, and often replies to questions with a grunt – that is when he is yanked forward, thrust into the limelight and put on the reading desk in front of a large crowd. To say it is a baptism of fire would be to mix religious metaphors, but it effectively tells him (and now her): "whatever you feel, you count, you are important, you have a role to play and we value you." It may not be cool for them to admit it, but there is no doubt that they are proud of themselves afterwards and feel a sense of achievement. It also links them into communal life and the chain of tradition, adding another link to it, with their name engraved on it.

Of course, not all children are educationally equipped to do what others do, and most synagogues will tailor the ceremony to the child, be it reading less verses or doing so in English. Some of the most moving occasions have been with those with severe learning difficulties. On one occasion, a child could not even read English and instead drew a picture of a Jewish scene and held it up proudly as I read from the scrolls on his behalf. In another instance, the child simply placed his hand on top of the pointer I was using to read the text, as if it was a joint venture. For them, it was as much an achievement as someone who had read the full portion themselves flawlessly. Of course, there can also be hiccups in what should be a joyous family event. One of the readings done by the thirteen-year-old is the Ten Commandments, and on a small number of occasions I have to keep my head down when he/she reaches "You shall not commit adultery" and make sure I am not inadvertently looking at someone. It was also the reason why the mother and father are seated not next to each other, but on opposite sides of the room, and so too are their respective families.

In many other cases, though, one of the intriguing things about a bar/batmitvah – and this may apply to a church confirmation too – is the significance for the parents. Quite apart from the pride they feel at their offspring's achievement, there is also a darker side. If they are saying their child is now coming of age and growing up, it also means that the child will be growing away from them. He or she will be less compliant, less reliant, more keen to experiment and wanting to make their own decisions. The parents have now lost their baby and are fast losing control too. It can also be a nerve-wracking time too, as the child emerges more independently into the wider world and all the potential slip-ups and dangers that the parents can foresee. It can be a steep learning curve for the parents: the child has had to learn his/her portion, but the parents have the even more difficult task of letting go, gradually stepping back and allowing the child to go off to make his/her own discoveries and mistakes. That can be hard for even the most loving and well-adjusted mum and dad. It is also a marker for them in terms of their own lives. If their child is now thirteen, it means the parents are no longer in their twenties, or even their thirties, but are fast approaching middle age. There is nothing wrong with that, but it can be a wake-up call about the passing of time, its effect on them, whether they are living the way they want to, and how they wish to use the years that lie ahead.

One instance where parental letting-go went wrong was the case of a barmitzvah when the mother took her son to buy a new suit. They tried on two and, despite his protests, she bought the one she liked and he did not. He had objected at the time, but she had ignored him, and he objected further on the day as the family got ready to leave home. He was incensed that, as he saw it, it was about his mother exerting control over "her little boy", as well as showing off to all the friends she had invited. He was probably right. The result was when they arrived at the synagogue, he went straight to the back garden and refused to come inside. His parents were distraught and told me he said he was not going ahead with the barmitzvah, presumably because he was too overwhelmed at speaking in public. When I realised what was happening, I went out to have a chat with him, and after some detective work, got to the root of the problem: not nerves, but vengeance. We talked over who else he would be hurting if he did not proceed, along with ways of making his parents appreciate that they had to start treating him differently and consulting his opinion more. It worked in two senses: he came inside, and when his brother had his barmitzvah two years later, he got to choose his own suit.

A problem that applies to every pupil is how to make their ceremony as meaningful as possible, rather than a rote recital of Hebrew. An innovation that I stumbled upon proved a success – taking bar/batmitzvah students to football matches. It came about because one of my sons and I are ardent Reading fans, go regularly to matches and each have a season ticket. However, once his career developed, his work commitments meant that he was busy on some Saturday afternoons. What should I do with his spare ticket on those occasions? At first I took assorted friends, but then I hit on the idea on taking bar/batmitvah pupils. Some turned down the offer in horror – rabbis are for synagogue, not for fun – but others were very pleased to accept, especially if they had never been to a football match before. (What wicked parents for ignoring such an important part of their general education!) It was also a treat for those from poorer homes who could not afford the ticket price and overall cost of such an outing. A parent would drop the child off at my house and off we went. Going there and back gave me a chance to chat outside of the classroom context, get to know them better and also talk about Jewish life in ways more relevant to them personally. The only problem arose when, as a result of growing revelations about child abuse scandals within the Church, the health and safety officer said that it was no longer appropriate for me to be alone with a child in a car. Instead, they would have to meet me at the stadium, where having 25,000 others around us made it a safe environment, and the parents pick up the child from there afterwards. Not only did this take away a lot of the conversation time together, but it meant that those families who did not have a car, or who were working all day Saturday and could not bring their child, had to miss out completely. I totally understood the rationale for the ruling, but resented the fact that it penalised children of less well-off families. I still do it for those who can come, though I am saddened that the fear of what might go wrong has ended up limiting the enjoyment of those who might benefit most.

Chapter 4

Match

Mating

My comments on weddings may upset some people but it is better to come clean and be honest. I have two less-than-euphoric confessions about them. In the interests of a religious health warning, I should point out that I am not speaking on behalf of all rabbis, though I suspect many feel the same. The first issue is that, although I am very glad they happen and although they are very joyous events, they are hard work. There is a great deal of paperwork to do, more than any other cycle-of-life ceremony. This is exacerbated by the fact that I am also a Marriage Registrar (as are many, but not all, ministers). This entails more form-filling on behalf of the State, but does allow me to conduct a wedding wherever I want (or, rather, wherever the couple want), be it in synagogue, hotel grounds, at their home or up a tree-house. More complicated, though, are the details of the service, such as which readings to add, the music to be played, who will stand where, and who will say what. On the one hand, I am keen that the couple get the ceremony that reflects them and is not the factory line service; on the other hand, this can involve endless discussions and me forcing them to come to a decision. Of course, as it is often the first wedding they have undertaken, that is not entirely surprising, but for me it may be the two hundredth (and sometimes not even the only one I am doing that same day), so my patience is not quite as elastic as theirs!

An added complication in this respect is that it is not just the couple making the decisions. Behind them stand an army of relatives, with their own opinions, if not demands, as well as a list of expectations, some of which are either unrealistic or contradictory (e.g., a "very intimate ceremony", but with a hundred and eighty guests), not to mention a determination that "long-standing family traditions" (which, in truth, can be just the last wedding they attended) be observed. The scene is set for a pre-marital blood-bath and many a couple admit that they consider eloping at some point. The biggest service I can do for the couple is to remind them that it is their wedding, not someone else's, and that all those "we-only-have-your-best-interest-at heart" advisers had their turn when it was their ceremony and should let the couple decide theirs for themselves. Actually, this is not entirely true, as there was a generational hiccup when there was a switch from couples whose wedding was largely paid for and controlled by their parents, then had offspring who expected to arrange their own ceremony and be free of any constraints. Those in the middle of the switch neither got to organise their own wedding, nor that of their children, and felt miffed that they had missed out. Despite that, I have no compunction in telling the couple that they should go ahead with a format they want, but to which their relatives object, and that I am happy to speak to the latter if that would help. There is nothing more dispiriting than officiating at what is supposed to be a couple's big day when you know it is not what they want at all.

My second confession about weddings – again, personal to me, but I know some other colleagues feel the same – is that I prefer officiating at funerals. This is not out of any sense of ghoulishness or dislike of people enjoying themselves – there are few experiences more heartwarming than seeing a couple in love setting out on a bright new future together – but from a rabbi's perspective, we can be more useful at funerals. A wedding will almost always be a stunning success however badly the rabbi mangles the service. The joy of the couple, the beaming faces of family and the whoops of friends will characterise the day and dominate the reminiscences. Except in some special instances, the rabbi is irrelevant, a mere cypher to the proceedings. At a funeral, however, there is a much more pro-active role to play and the emotions of those attending have a greater range and intensity, be they grief, numbness, anger, guilt, bewilderment, sense of abandonment, family rifts, succession battles or religious questioning. The way the rabbi conducts the service, involves mourners, addresses issues both obvious and unspoken, reconciles different factions, gives comfort and offers a way forward out of the morass can be crucial. It can make the difference between a funeral that is healing, or that is inconsequential, or that is even counter-productive and exacerbates the problems faced by the mourners. The emotional stakes are much higher at a funeral than a wedding, and the ability of the rabbi to help or blunder is much greater.

Still, there is one enormous question mark that rabbis and other clergy have to face at a wedding that does need some delicacy. What happens if you think the marriage will not work? Do you say so? Do you refuse to officiate? Or do you supress your personal opinion? Getting married is one of the biggest gambles a person ever undertakes in life. They are binding themselves to a person they may not know as well as they think, and linking their future to someone who may change. They are also promising that their own feelings towards the other person will remain the same for several decades to come, guaranteeing their emotions in advance. It is no wonder that so many marriages end in failure and that the divorce rate is so high. At the same time, precisely because human chemistry is so hard to predict, it can be dangerous territory for the rabbi to do that. I have seen marriages that I was convinced were made in heaven turn sour and crash down. Equally, those that I privately thought had little chance of reaching their second anniversary are still going happily after thirty years.

But do ministers have a moral duty to voice opinions if they think problems lie ahead? I have done so only in a few cases, taking the attitude that it is legitimate to at least raise questions for the couple to consider, and then accept their answer. But even grounds for concern that seem obvious can prove mistaken. I did ask a couple who had a twenty-five-year age gap between them if they had thought about the long-term consequences. I referred, as gently as I could, to energy levels in bringing up children, or the effect of time when one of them approached possible deterioration at eighty and the other was still a healthy fifty-five. They told me in no uncertain terms that they had. In fact, they were right and have had a long and happy marriage. I was glad to be wrong, but, despite being embarrassed at asking, would have felt much worse if I had not done so and the marriage had ended in tears.

In this particular case, the couple had thought through the issues that lay ahead, but it is surprising how many do not. Reverse priorities rule the day. Enormous energy goes into planning the four or five hours of the wedding, but not the forty or fifty years that lie ahead. This led me to establish an annual marriage preparation evening at which I gathered all couples together who were planning to wed that year. It had a dual function, firstly to get couples facing similar issues to meet each other, compare notes and share experiences. Secondly, we looked beyond the wedding day and discussed what marriage meant. This also included answering twenty questions I set them about how well they knew each other, which they had to fill out separately and then see how accurate they were. Questions included whether the other person wanted children (and, if so, how many), the saddest moment of their life up till then, whether they prefer to build up savings or spend what they earn, and what special family traditions they have which they want to continue.

Most people score fifteen out of twenty, with a few amusing errors; but for those who obtain less than ten, it acts as a wake-up call to delve deeper into the person to whom they are about to commit themselves. There is also one trick question: "What would you most like to change about him/her?" The only right answer is "I won't try." In other words, marriage is about accepting the person as they are, and attempts to remould them imply a dissatisfaction that should ring alarm bells. In addition, except for some superficial habits (like not putting the loo seat down after use, or leaving the toothpaste top open), the attempts usually fail, as most people do not change their essential characteristics.

There have only been two cases when I told a couple outright that they should not continue their relationship. One was a mixed-faith couple. In the vast majority of those in a similar position whom I have counselled, even though there are cultural and religious issues to overcome, there has usually been enough room for manoeuvre and willingness to find compromises for the relationship to succeed. This particular couple were clearly in love, but also had diametrically opposed views of how to run their future home together and how to bring up any children. It was quite distressing to see the mismatch between their genuine affection for each other and any route forward together. I felt obliged to tell them that, of the around three thousand mixed-faith couples I had encountered, they were the only ones I felt should not go ahead. They were very upset, but it was also clear that, as can often be the case, they knew deep down that what I was saying was right, but had never had the courage to say it aloud to themselves.

This can often be an important role for the rabbi, in a multiplicity of situations: bringing to the surface difficult thoughts or articulating what people were feeling, but not expressing. It can apply to conversations about a well-established marriage that had effectively ended without anyone admitting it, or to the need for a career move after years of stagnation. It can also be our role when someone is terminally ill, but no one in the family is willing to confront that reality and the consequences for them. Equally, it can be speaking with the person concerned and asking questions that the family had been nervous of asking in case it upsets him/her, or which they themselves find difficult, but which, actually, the person might wish to talk about. Questions phrased in a way that do not tell the person they are dying if they do not already know, or do not wish to know, but that still allow him/her to talk about their feelings or fears. These might be: Are you afraid? Is there anything you want to discuss? What is bothering you most at this moment? Those who wish to avoid talking about death will make it immediately clear through their answer, and the conversation quickly moves on to other topics, but those who do want to explore any aspect of their mortality will seize the opportunity.

The other engaged couple with whom I voiced misgivings were two individuals, each of whom I had known before they met each other. Both were lovely people and I was delighted for them when they told me they wished to get married. My doubts arose when we met to talk about the wedding day, and then increased markedly at the marriage preparation session. They did not agree on much, had very different approaches and saw the future in contrasting ways. When I pointed this out, I was told that all was well and they were heading in the same direction. A subsequent conversation led me to strongly doubt this. I reiterated my discomfort at their lack of togetherness and suggested they might want to give themselves some extra time to get to know each other better and set a later date for the wedding. They declined, assured me all was fine and the wedding went ahead as planned. Three months later they separated.

When I spoke to the wife after their split, I tried to avoid any hint of "I-told-you-so" and merely asked what she thought had gone wrong. The answer was brutally honesty. She said that she had known that the marriage was not right for her, but had felt trapped in the engagement process (planning the food, the guest list, the wedding dress), as well as the weight of expectation of family and friends. "I reckoned it was easier to go ahead and get divorced quietly afterwards, than cause a major upset by calling the wedding off," she told me. She also preferred the status of a young divorcee, rather than being a single woman left on the shelf or jilted. On the one hand, it would have been far better to have been honest with her fiancé at the time than to go through with what was effectively a sham wedding, not to mention both the emotional cost and financial expense. On the other hand, I understood the logic of her thinking, and the way that individuals can feel they lose control once the engagement is announced and they are railroaded along from then on.

I did tell her that she should have spoken to someone before the wedding, be it me or anyone else in whom she could have confided and discussed the options, but I did not feel it was right to rant and rage at her. There was no point after the event, while there were plenty of other people doing that already. What she needed from me was some support in forging a way out of the mess. Curiously enough, this is where we did fall out, as she reckoned that she did not need to return the wedding presents, as they were given voluntarily. I took the attitude that they were received under false pretences and should be handed back. I think she felt that, having lost so much in the debacle, she wanted to hold onto some material gains. I did manage to persuade her to relinquish them – if for no other reason than to avoid a trail of angry people cursing her name – though I know she was sorely tempted to keep two or three that she liked best.

The wedding day

As for the actual wedding ceremony, there have been many changes in the service compared to those forty years ago. Some couples add some extra music, such as the bride entering to a pop song or modern Israeli folk tune. They may also write their own marriage vow to make it more intimate. Family and friends might be more involved, such as by reading the *Sheva B'rachot*, the Seven Wedding Blessings, rather than the rabbi doing them. Occasionally, instead of the groom stamping on the glass at the end of the ceremony, they will both do so (although I usually suggest they each have a separate glass to stamp on, lest they start stepping on each other's toes too early on in the marriage). I always have to supress the instinct to make the quip "this custom signifies it is the last time the groom can put his foot down" – partly because it is so hackneyed and partly because it now feels very sexist (even though it may sometimes still be true). I also avoid giving the traditional explanation that the rite dates back to mourning the destruction of the Temple in Jerusalem in the first century and how we grieve for the many tragedies that have befallen our people. To be honest, I do not think a couple or their guests care very much about what the Roman legions did to us two thousand years ago. Also, I much prefer to give a modern interpretation that feels more relevant: that it signifies that every relationship has the sound of stamping feet and breaking glass, but a good marriage is where the arguments are resolved and the joys shared.

Usually I collect up the shattered pieces after the ceremony (the glass is wrapped in a napkin so as not to send vicious shards hurtling towards the guests) and bin them whilst everyone is hugging and taking photographs. This proved to be a heinous crime as far as one family was concerned for, unbeknown to me, they had the tradition that the pieces were then put in a velvet bag and kept by the front door as a permanent reminder of their marriage. Apparently, I had now ruined their happiness. Personally, I am not sure that broken glass is the best symbol to keep as a memento, and I would have thought that the wedding ring or having the *ketubah* (the Hebrew marriage certificate, a technical document but often illustrated beautifully) hanging on the wall would be more appropriate. For the record, though, that particular marriage has survived despite my error. Other couples have been known to use the pieces to make an artistic design that is then framed, or to fashion a *mezuzah,* the Jewish symbol that goes on one's front door. At one wedding at which I presided, the groom took five attempts to smash the glass, getting more and more embarrassed each time as he desperately tried to impress his new wife and guests. It is not supposed to be a macho test, but a groom who does not do it first time rarely forgets.

A more common problem with which rabbis have to contend is the official photographer. I am sure they used to be more restrained, standing still at a discreet distance and only too grateful to be allowed in. Now they seem to regard the wedding ceremony as their domain, obsessive at capturing each moment and have no compunction at wandering in and out of the canopy during the service. I have learnt to make it my first task on arriving at the venue to meet the photographer and let him or her – even worse, it is sometimes two of them, so that they cover every angle – know what I will and will not tolerate. I feel as if I am about to enter a jousting match, facing an opponent who is set upon outright victory, while I am equally determined to win the day. Usually we manage to reach a compromise, with the photographer getting the key shots they want, and me ensuring they are not prancing around and a major distraction. On one occasion, the parley broke down and the photographer started weaving his way between the bride and groom. I did not want to have a row and ruin the ceremony, but nor did I want him squirming around us. I stopped for a moment, and whispered, as thunderously as I could whilst smiling, that one of us had to leave immediately. His lance clattered broken to the ground and he slid away. Phew!

Nowadays, the photographer has been joined by the video operator, who also wants the best shots, but I have generally managed to banish him/her to a fixed position on a tripod. Then there are the guests themselves. In the days of cameras, it was only one or two individuals who brought one along, stood up in the middle of the service to take a picture, and of course block the view of those sitting behind them as well as making clicking noises. Now, everyone has their mobile with them and reckons that unless they capture the moment on their phone, it is as if it did not exist. Before the service starts, I announce that the only photos to be taken during the service will be that of the official photographer, but all those present will have a chance to have plenty at the end. I still sense that they feel I am undermining their basic right to snap at will but, to be fair, most people do abide by it. A rabbinic glare is usually sufficient to warn off any miscreants, and very occasionally a rabbinic finger pointing at them is needed to stop repeat offenders. It may be a joyous wedding, but there is also a hard-fought war going on underneath the surface.

There can also be a few own-goals when the couple's spectacular plans go wrong. In one case, the bride and groom were determined to have maximum privacy, so holding it at a hotel or synagogue where other people might be around was out. Nor did they want it too near a road in case the noise of cars destroyed the atmosphere they were carefully cultivating. They reckoned they had found the perfect solution by going to a private restaurant on an island in the Thames where they could be guaranteed exclusive access. It was a beautiful day, the sun shone, the water sparkled and the wedding seemed to be heading towards perfection. Suddenly there was roar of engines and a loud "Cor, it's a wedding – don't it look lovely!" which boomed out. They had forgotten about boats passing by. In addition, we were not too far away from a lock, so it was not just one boat but a whole succession of them as they all came out together. The day-trippers stood on the deck waving, taking photos and shouting what they thought were encouraging messages. The couple were mortified. I thought of saying something soothing like "better luck next time", but quickly realised that, ideally, there should not be a next time and restricted myself to nodding sympathetically.

Another incident was when a wedding took place in the garden of a hotel that was alongside the river. Everyone was assembled outside, waiting for the ceremony to begin, except for the bride and her father. The guests looked towards the hotel entrance, expecting to see her car drive up, when suddenly someone shouted: "Look, there she is!" and pointed to a boat gliding towards them, with the bride looking radiant on the deck. It was indeed a glorious sight. People clapped as the boat moored alongside the riverbank perfectly. Then disaster struck. They had planned everything in advance, except for the fact that there was a very slight gap between the riverbank and the boat, owing to the fender protecting it. Normally, this would not be a problem and merely required a small step across it. However, it just so happened that the bride was wearing an extremely tight dress which impeded her leg movements and meant she could not make the step across. She was unable to get ashore and stood helpless on the deck. In the end, it was resolved by two of the guests getting onto the boat, standing either side of her and, as elegantly as they could, lifting her up and plonking her on the riverbank. It won them a round of applause, although there was one person who was guffawing away more than I thought seemly. He got his comeuppance, for as he was bending over in laughter, the camera he was wearing round his neck slipped out of its case and into the river. Splash! Now who was red-faced?

Living together

There is one definite sociological change surrounding marriage. When I first started as a rabbi, all the couples filling out the forms gave separate addresses for each partner. Even if they were already sharing the same one, they still felt obliged to pretend not to be, and would use their parents' home as cover. Now it is extraordinarily unusual for them not to be living together, while they all put down the same address on the Marriage Registry form. At one point, the period of living together as husband and wife, but not being legally wed, was called "a trial marriage", but now it has just become the way things happen. Within the Jewish community, most couples living together do eventually get married, be it between two and eight years later. What is noticeable, though, is that this has not lessened the divorce rate. That is strange: one would have thought that the couple had got to know each other well enough to have sorted out whether they had a long-term future or not. But maybe there are explanations for this apparent discrepancy: some couples may have got into a rut and assumed all was well when it was not; some may have been going through problems and thought that getting married would solve them; some may have felt it was simply too hard to disentangle the joint mortgage and furniture by that stage and hoped for the best. There was one couple, though, whom I inadvertently upset. I noticed that they had put down separate addresses. When we met to discuss the wedding, I asked (so as to get to know more about them) if they were nevertheless living together and they said "no". When I asked "how come not?" – partly out of surprise, partly out of genuine interest – they said they were shocked at the suggestion. I thought they might walk out and look for a more conservative rabbi, but they stayed put and everything proceeded smoothly. There are also couples who have not only been cohabiting, but have already got young children. In these instances, it is not uncommon for them to act as the pageboys and bridesmaids. Charming or alarming, either way it is a sign of changing times.

There was only one couple who I turned away. I did not know them, as they were not members of the synagogue, but they rang up, said they were living in the area and wished to get married. The interview went fine and it seemed it would be a relatively uncomplicated ceremony. Then, at the very end,

I asked my usual question: "Is there anything we have not covered that you would like to mention?" They looked at each other and then said, "Actually, yes, we were wondering if we could include the *Our Father* prayer in the service?" I gulped. There is nothing wrong with the prayer, but it is a Christian one. Why did they want it? After some initial hesitation, they admitted they were Jews for Jesus. This is a very small group of Jews in Britain who have accepted Jesus as the Messiah, but still regard themselves as Jews and see their new belief as a fulfilment of their Judaism, not a departure from it. The problem is that although Judaism and Christianity share much on an ethical level, the clear dividing line between them is Jesus: to us, he was a gifted preacher, to them he is the Son of God. The couple may have seen themselves as Jewish, but to me (and most other rabbis), they have effectively become Christian. I have no objection to them changing faith if that is what brings them spiritual happiness, but for me they are no longer Jewish. That matters, as I am only empowered by the State to marry two people "both professing the Jewish faith". I wished them well, but had to abandon the plans for their marriage. I thought that was the end of the matter until I heard that they had subsequently got married at an Orthodox synagogue. I was surprised, as the latter are associated with being much stricter over protocols, but the couple had been canny: this time they did not mention any special requests and the wedding went ahead.

On another occasion, I was the lenient one. A couple came to me to get married, but first had a tale to tell. Her husband had had a stroke, resulting in him being in a permanent coma. She had visited him daily in hospital, but after some years had become close to someone else and they had moved in together. She had still continued visiting her husband and did not let the new relationship affect her care for him. When he died, she and her partner decided to get married and hence the visit. Technically, I should have refused to discuss anything further with them, as they had committed adultery and Jewish law stipulates that a person may not marry their paramour. However, it seemed to me that she had still been a dutiful wife, as much as she could in the circumstances, while just because the husband was in a coma was no reason why she should have been denied the chance for happiness with someone else. True, she would have faced a dilemma if he had suddenly recovered whilst she was living with the other person, but I had no doubt that she would have put her husband first. I went ahead with the marriage.

I was spared a similar paramour case, when a congregant came home early one day to find his wife in bed with another man. He was also married and it resulted in both couples getting divorces. In the course of the divorce proceedings, my congregant came to get friendly with the other man's wife, they struck up a relationship, and now wanted to get married. As it happened, so did the two who had committed the adultery, meaning that the two couples had ended up swopping partners. Fortunately, it was the "innocent couple" who came to me and I had no hesitation in conducting the ceremony. In case you are wondering what would have happened if it was the "guilty couple" who had approached me, then I would have had to do some soul-searching. Whilst Jewish law does ban paramours from marrying – to discourage adulterers benefitting from a misdemeanour – Reform rabbis have qualified this depending on the circumstances. Did the adultery break up an otherwise stable marriage (in which case, we will not go ahead), or was it a symptom of a marriage that had already died (in which case, we will)? It is a fine line to tread, but it is a more humane response than a blanket ban. The distinction was originally introduced for couples who were still legally married, but had been living apart for a while and who had formed new relationships pending a divorce. Might it also sometimes apply to a couple still sharing the same home, as in the above case? Undoubtedly, there are couples who are married and living together, but whose marriage is effectively over. That does not justify the adultery, but can explain it and mitigate the subsequent consequences. Who said rabbis live in an ivory tower!

Despite unusual cases such as the above, what has repeatedly caught me by surprise are much more mundane instances. A couple move into the area and join the synagogue. They have been married for several years and have children, and it seems a very loving relationship and stable home. Then it transpires, they are both divorced and this is a second marriage. With a high divorce rate at present, this should not be at all surprising, yet I still get a jolt to think that had I known them a decade earlier, I would not be encountering a happy family. Instead there would be two individuals, both in the midst of painful marriages that were in their death throes, with mutual recriminations and legal fights permeating the air. I am genuinely pleased that they have come through such a horrible experience and found happiness with someone else. It shows that whereas we always hope that a marriage will last forever and celebrate each wedding joyously, it is sometimes the second marriages that are the better marriages.

In one person's case, though, it has turned out that her third marriage has proved to be the best one. Moreover, I officiated at all three of her weddings. Some congregants might have thought it was bad luck to have the same person conduct the ceremony, or maybe slightly embarrassing that I had witnessed two past failures, but she was up for it and so was I. Still, it did take a lot of self-control not to ad lib something like "Here we go again" or "Third time lucky, eh?" It certainly reminds me how grateful I am that we do not have in the Jewish wedding that famous, but unrealistic, line: "Till death us do part". Whereas the New Testament viewed marriage vows as sacrosanct and unbreakable, the Hebrew Bible saw divorce as an option – a sadness, but not a sin. The rabbis have always continued that tradition, stating that, on the one hand, the heavens shed a tear every time a relationship broke down, but that, on the other hand, marriage should not be a prison. If, for whatever reason, a mistake had been made or a rupture occurred, then there was no reason why people should be locked together in unhappiness.

Personally, I feel that the presence of children can strengthen the case for an unhappy couple to get divorced, not weaken it, as some would suggest. I understand there is a certain nobility in "staying together for the sake of the children". If the couple can maintain a basic civility, and give each other freedom of manoeuvre without resentments building up, then it can be beneficial for children to have both parents under the same roof. However, if there is open hostility between the couple, and the home is full of screaming rows, then it is far better for the children to live with just one parent and be brought up in a calm atmosphere. There may be some financial consequences of a split that affect them, but at least the emotional cost will be less damaging.

What makes a marriage that will survive? Having been at both the starting point and finishing line of so many, I hesitate to use the word "love" as it is hard to define. It is always dependent on feelings, which can be highly unpredictable and subject to change. Something much firmer and more solid is needed. My preferred term is "partnership". An agreement to face the world and its challenges together, based on mutual respect and trust, as well as liking each other's company. This may sound transactional, but it can include both types of love: the high-octane passionate love on first encounter, and the love that grows over time as the experience of each other deepens. The latter is evident from the way the Bible describes Isaac's relationship with Rebecca: that he met her, and married her, and came to love her (Genesis 24.67). In some marriages, I can point to a shared cultural background that makes them eminently suitable for each other; in others, they come from totally different worlds, but still fit perfectly. Some partners are very similar to each other and share the same niche; others are completely opposite characters and complement each other wonderfully. Despite the heartache of marriages that fail, the benefits of those that succeed, means that it is still worth pursuing, and rabbis are there for both, like marshals along the route of a running race, trying to help them complete the course but there to help if not.

I certainly do not subscribe to the view that there is such a person as Mr Right (or Mrs Right), just one person who can be your perfect partner. I am very sure that there are several, probably dozens of them, and although the relationship might be slightly different, they will be equally fulfilling. But I am sad that so many people, who live alone and would much prefer not to do so, cannot meet someone appropriate for them. I know they would make loving husbands or wives, and would blossom if they were loved back, but a match never happens. Sometimes it is just bad luck; other times they can be too judgemental and dismiss people without getting to know them properly. There are also those who have been hurt in a previous relationship, do not want to risk it again and raise their emotional drawbridge, preventing anyone else from approaching. In yet more cases, it is because they fail to open themselves to social opportunities, just go to work, return home and draw the curtains. Unless they make the effort to join a bridge class, rambling group, book circle, political club, whatever, they will never allow themselves to meet new people. I know it is hard, but I also know that without it, they are condemning themselves to remaining alone.

It is one of the unofficial roles of a rabbi to create social events for single people to mix or to introduce people to each other. I am often asked, "Can you find someone nice for my son/daughter?" The only difference over the years has been that initially it was when the son/daughter was in their twenties, which was then felt to be "on the shelf". Nowadays they are more likely to be in their forties – either because people are getting married much later, or because they have already been married and are now divorced and looking for the next partner. Just for the record, and despite the above, when I am conducting a wedding I do not tell the bride that she is about to marry one of numerous Mr Rights who would have made her happy, nor do I speak to them about "the transaction" they are about to enter. Love is still the master of ceremonies. I also have a strong affection, which I share with some couples, for the rabbinic legend from the book of Jewish mysticism, the Zohar, that before a soul comes down to earth, it is split into two halves, male and female. The male half is then born as a boy, and the female half as a girl. True mating is when the two halves are joined together again in marriage. Who said I was not a romantic at heart!

I am not often invited to officiate at celebrity weddings, with my nearest occasions being that of the then chairman of Sainsbury's or the daughter of Frankie Vaughan. Fortunately, neither was over-glitzy and concentrated on the family, not the fame. With this in mind, I decided to turn down the one megastar occasion that came my way. Uri Geller and his wife, who were living nearby in Sonning, had decided to repeat their marriage vows and have a special ceremony of re-consecration. The guest list would be filled with famous personalities, while the best man was to be Michael Jackson. I was asked to co-officiate along with Rabbi Shmuley Boteach. Part of me felt it would be a memorable event and one to reminisce over for many years. But I also thought it might turn into a media circus that would become more and more excruciating. There was also a problem with timing, as it was set for a Friday afternoon and I was worried about possible delays. Shmuley could stay at the house if the reception spilled over into the Sabbath, but I had to get back to lead a service. Thank goodness I turned it down! I heard afterwards that it was impossible to get in or out of Sonning, as the police closed off the local roads to avoid unwanted guests, while the real ones arrived by helicopter in Uri's garden. Even if I had got a police escort out of the village, there was the additional problem that Michael Jackson came several hours late and the wedding was held up until he arrived. So I never met Michael, he never met me, but the service at Maidenhead Synagogue started on time that Friday evening.

Chapter 5

Scratch

Sex

There are two views about rabbis and sex. One is that we are a source of authority on all matters and there is no subject upon which we cannot be consulted. This goes back to the key rabbinic text of the second century, the Mishnah, which, amongst many other topics, discusses the times when a husband and wife can or cannot have sexual intercourse, and which goes into minute details about the size of a bloodspot that will determine whether or not the wife is menstruating. Nothing that affects the life of Jews is alien to the rabbinic remit. The other view is from a much later period and would not dream of raising such base issues with a man of piety. I suspect this is influenced more by wider society and a combination of the other-worldly image of vicars, however unfair that is, along with the abiding influence of Victorian attitudes. Sex may be flaunted publicly on television or in billboard advertisements, but is still a topic many feel embarrassed to talk about, especially when it comes to their own performance. Today, much depends on the vibes that a rabbi gives off. In a previous book, *Confessions of a Rabbi*, I detailed various problems to do with sex that people had discussed with me. One of my colleagues was genuinely mystified and said: "None of my congregants ever talk about sex with me." Perhaps it is also a matter of us picking up signals or asking the right questions. When someone told me that she and her husband were having difficulties, I asked, "Is that in bed or out of bed?" It meant the conversation then took a totally different turn from if I had said "Are you finding it hard to communicate?" Of course, there are many things other than sex that can go wrong in a marriage, but my response was a way of indicating that we could discuss all of them and without any no-go areas.

An example of this was Phil and Maddy (not their real names), who always seemed fairly happy when they came to synagogue, be it for a service or social event. As is so often the case, though, people who would not dream of going on stage can still be wonderful actors and actresses, covering up their true emotions and presenting a public image of how they would like to be, rather than how they are. In their case, I only got to know the truth when Phil rang me to say he was in trouble and could I come round. It turned out that Maddy had decided to leave and rent a flat near to her parents' home. When I asked why, he said she had told him she wanted her independence. I sensed from the way he had said this that something important was missing. So I asked a question that might have gone horribly wrong but turned out to be the right one: "And the real reason?" It took a while to emerge, but it turned out that they had never consummated the marriage. They had slept in the same bed and been on good terms, but simply not had sex together. He had not initiated it, and she, perhaps feeling abashed at the subject or that she was not attractive enough to warrant it, had not requested it or commented on its absence. After a while, it had become such a well-established pattern – saying good night, putting out the light and turning over – that it was easier to stick to it than change anything or even discuss it. Phil still valued the marriage and enjoyed her company, and had thought that she felt the same. However, a row the previous week over a relatively insignificant matter had snowballed into the larger issue of their relationship as a whole, in which Maddy became increasingly emotional and that culminated in her saying: "And it's not as if we are even properly married, so I don't know why I am bothering to argue with you." I suggested the obvious steps – going to marriage guidance counselling, as well as seeing a sex therapist – but it never happened. The following year, his pharmaceutical company offered him a transfer to Switzerland on a three-year contract, which he accepted and he eventually made it his permanent home.

I have often noticed that "truth is stranger than fiction" when it comes to matters of the heart (or the genitals). That saying may be a cliché, but clichés usually arise because they are truisms that are repeated based on experience. We had one congregant who ran off with his mother-in-law, which was doubly awful for his wife, as she lost both a husband and mother at the same time. In another case, a young couple in their twenties rented a room in the home of an older couple in their early forties. A few months later, the young woman ran off with the older husband, and the young man moved into the bedroom of his abandoned wife. In another instance, during a coach trip to the Lake District for young couples, a husband and wife in different marriages sat next to each other as they wanted to use the time to discuss a synagogue project on which they were both working. Unfortunately, the journey inspired something else in them, and by the time we got back, they decided to stay on together, resulting in two divorces.

Meanwhile, Becky and Julian had been married for ten years when she fell pregnant and gave birth to Dina (all names changed). Julian was not at all pleased at her arrival as he was infertile, and so she had clearly been the product of an affair. In fact, the marriage broke up shortly afterwards, they divorced and Becky married Dina's actual father. However, for the sake of saving face, Julian never revealed to anyone else that he was infertile and it remained known only to the four of them. Several years later, Julian remarried someone who already had children and was past child-bearing age. Around a decade later, Julian was diagnosed with Huntingdon's Disease, from which he eventually died. His second wife, who never knew he was infertile, telephoned Dina to alert her to the situation, as well as to warn her that it was a hereditary disease and that she should have regular check-ups herself. Although they had hardly ever spoken before, Dina responded politely and then chatted about her father's condition. After putting the phone down, she told me later, she cried out: "Thank God he wasn't my actual dad after all!"

Another curious case concerned a widower who was in his seventies but remarkably fit, slender and a keen tennis player. He and his wife had lived abroad for many years as tax exiles, but after she died he returned to England and settled in this area. On the first anniversary of his wife's death, I had a chat with him and asked how he was managing and how he coped with being alone. He looked at me with a glint in his eye and said "Don't worry, rabbi, I get what I want." I was referring to his emotional needs, not anything else, but I left it at that. However, I recalled the conversation a couple of years later when he died from a heart attack and his body had to be collected from the massage parlour where it had occurred. I wondered whether it was indeed a massage parlour or if it was a "massage parlour". Either way, I hope he died a happy man.

I am sure we do not have any more scandals than any other congregation, though it could be said that "there is something in the air" locally. Maidenhead was well known in Edwardian times as near enough to London for men to visit their mistresses, but close enough to be back in time for dinner. The hotel "Skindles" and the accommodation along Horseguards Parade (very indicative of the male tenants in that area) carried a certain reputation in earlier days, and led to the ironic line "Are You Married or Do You Live in Maidenhead?" In addition, Cliveden is just up the road, the country house still famous (or infamous) for the Profumo affair, which helped bring down the Macmillan government in 1963.

Amid all these sexual comings and goings, there can also be love without sex. One twenty-eight-year-old wife confided in me that when she found she was infertile, she went off sex.

Her husband was content to abstain, but worried that this might affect their relationship. Once she told him she was happy to hold hands, cuddle and have other types of physical contact, he was reassured and their marriage is now reaching its fortieth anniversary. Conversely, another husband found he lost his ability to have an erection in middle age and declined to take any treatment to restore it. When I asked how his wife had reacted and whether she felt she was missing out on sex with him, he replied: "Oh, she's fine! When I broke the news to her, she told me she had lost interest in sex after we had children, and although we continued to have sex, apparently she was only doing it for my sake. So now both of us don't want sex and we are happy without it."

Temptation

It is only fair that, in a chapter on sex, I mention not only the laity, but clergy too. There is an incendiary danger faced by ministers of all faith: temptation. Looking back, it is astonishing that this was never mentioned during my rabbinic training. Were my teachers – largely congregational rabbis themselves – so ethereal that they never noticed, or so unappealing no one ever approached them? But as our work is often on a one-to-one basis, the chance that someone will find you attractive, be you a bright young thing or a person of experience, is bound to happen every now and then. I recall a routine visit I did to a woman who was dressed very ordinarily, so much so that I hardly noticed the skirt and top she was wearing, and we chatted about the community for around half an hour. We had been sitting in separate armchairs on one side of a large room, which had less light than the other side, which was dominated by three big windows. After a while, she stood up and moved to the window side, standing in front of them facing me, legs astride and hands on hips. With the light now behind her I realised her top was see-through, as was her skirt. "So, what happens now?" she said invitingly. It was time to leave!

I do not want to suggest that such situations are a weekly occurrence – and although being viewed as a sex symbol can be very flattering, it would be mentally exhausting if it was constant – but they do happen periodically. Nor are they just a matter of physical attraction, but can also arise out of emotional closeness. If you have been a good listener and sympathetic support to someone who has been going through a traumatic period – such as a divorce or bereavement – they can come to view you not just as a first-rate minister, but as a kindred spirit. If, at the same time, you cross over from helping them to identifying with them, an affinity can grow that can lead to a mutual attachment. The border between a professional relationship and a personal one is thin, and it is easy for both parties to slip from one to the other. Even if the minister is always conscious of keeping his/her side of the boundary, the congregant may not be, resulting in mistaken assumptions or hurt feelings. Just as we have to control the urge to be rude to congregants who drive us bonkers, we have to perform the equally hard job of not being too nice to those we like or care for.

Still, as you may be thinking to yourself already, attraction is a two-way street. Just as we were never given any lessons in avoidance techniques, nor were we warned about self-control. God may be our boss, and there may be several mentions of "Thou shalt not" in our job spec, but human nature applies as much to rabbis as it does to double-glazed window salesmen or other door-to-door visitors. The only difference is that for us it means the sack, whereas that may not apply to them if they win an order. Despite the occasional lurid headline in the tabloids about a randy rabbi or voracious vicar, very few of them intended to have an affair at the beginning of that particular day. It was generally a mix of chance circumstance and natural inclinations that led to the liaison. Of course, being attracted to a person and jumping into bed with them are very different, but just because most ministers do not do the latter does not mean they do not feel the former. It is hard to pinpoint what is the most important factor in following morality rather than biology – fear of God, fear of one's partner's reaction, fear of their partner's reaction, fear of the overall consequences – but the combination of them all generally pulls us through tempting moments.

In all these situation, it is not just a matter of extracting oneself, but doing so without making the other person feel rejected, put down or embarrassed. When answering the question, "what would you like me to do for you?" – especially when said somewhat breathlessly by someone in a surprisingly low cut dress for an afternoon visit – then responding with "oh, a nice cup of tea, with milk and no sugar please" may mark me out as a dullard, but is a good way of refusing the other offer gently. The object is not just to maintain my moral purity, but to allow them to maintain their pride and still feel able to be part of the community. In almost all of the cases I can think of where this has been necessary, it was because of a momentary aberration on the part of the other person, rather than them being serial seducers. In fact, if any of them happen to be reading this right now, they would probably not even recognise themselves.

While we are being so frank with each other, perhaps I ought to confess that I have discovered another preventative harness to going astray: ageing. After reaching a certain decade, though this will vary from person to person, one is neither as attractive to others, nor as interested in others as before. There are many downsides to growing old and a declining libido is certainly one of them, but it does have its professional advantages. It may also be true that being a rabbi is one of the few jobs where the increasing years can enhance one's reputation. With many other jobs, in which fast-moving technological changes occur, being over a certain age means you are pre-historic. Hopefully, like a wine that matures, we grow wiser and more respected (providing, of course, we had not let temptation, infuriating congregants or other pitfalls derail us before reaching that point).

Divorce

As I intimated above, Judaism has always allowed divorce. My grandfather used to say, though it may not be original to him, "better an end with pain, than pain without end." I have only twice encountered an amicable divorce. Many start off that way, with the couple deciding in a measured way that they are not right for each other and it is time to take separate paths. They remain calm with each other, navigate telling family and friends, and if there are any children, make sensible arrangements. However, they almost always then fall out over the financial details. Each one thinks they need more than the other is offering, or that they have contributed more to the marital pot than the other appreciates. I always tell divorcing couples to prepare for a horrendous period in the proceedings. The only question mark is whether it will sour relations permanently, or whether they will emerge on good terms once through it. What I find depressing is when a couple are so intent on punishing each other that everything is contested and fought over in court, at the cost of tens of thousands of pounds. They never seem to realise that the settlement over which they are arguing so fiercely is about to be considerably reduced through soaring legal fees. Perhaps like gamblers at a casino, they can see their pot disappearing and hope that one last throw will win it all back. It never does.

Of course, not all hiccups in the marriage lead to divorce.

It is wonderful how helpful basic marriage guidance sessions can be in some cases. It can help the couple steer through a bad patch caused by external events, such as a death in the family that has unexpected effects, or money problems that can undermine the domestic stability. Alternatively, it can tackle a problem between the couple themselves, such as lack of communication or unrealistic expectations which, once pointed out, can be resolved. I have not mentioned adultery, though I shall do so now, for although it would seem to be the most obvious reason for marriages breaking up, I have been surprised at how often this has not been the result. It certainly hurts the other partner deeply but they do not automatically send for the divorce lawyer. Instead, many are prepared to give the marriage a second chance. What intrigues me are the varied reasons behind the decision. For some, it is because the offending partner tells them that it was a dreadful mistake and they truly regret it, and their partner has the grace to accept it. For some, it is because they fundamentally believe that the marriage is worth preserving, so they are willing to overlook the betrayal. Others fear the financial consequences of divorce and reckon it is better to make the best of a bad situation. Yet others worry about being alone, or hate the stigma of divorce, and so stay put. Still, this is only half the story, and for those who feel the marriage is now untenable, the divorce is usually much more rancorous than in other instances.

As rabbi, I am usually the first port of call. This might be because they value my counselling skills or because I am cheaper than a solicitor. I always make it clear that I am not a marriage guidance expert, but I can help with some basic untangling of what is the problem (sometimes they each identify a separate one and so have been arguing about solutions that the other thinks is irrelevant). I can get each partner to explain how they see it (and, more importantly, force the other one to listen until they have finished). I have also found it helpful to ask a question that catches both of them by surprise: when did you last make love? From the look on their face, I can see them thinking: "What! Are you really asking what I thought I heard you asking?" Despite the initial sharp intake of breath, they always tell me. It is not that I am being intrusive, but I have found that it says a lot about the relationship and helps get to the core of the issue very quickly. If it was in the last month, it may indicate a basic intimacy that is still present and a foundation upon which to build if they can find a way of being in harmony out of bed as much as in bed. If the answer is "four years ago", it tends to reveal a distancing that is now deeply embedded and a gulf that is much harder to bridge. Of course, this is assuming it was mutual love-making, not enforced sex. It is also not a foolproof litmus test, because lust can hide incompatibility; but it can be a useful barometer of what is going on beneath the surface differences.

There are cases where there is no chance of reconciliation. The husband who left his wife for his mother-in-law would never be allowed back, even if he wanted it. The multiple layers of hurt were enormous: the wife lost not only her husband, but her mother; amid her grief-cum-fury, she also had to console her bereft father, while the children lost both Daddy and Grandma at the same time. More common, but equally beyond repair, is when the husband leaves for another man, or the wife for a woman. Once unheard of, this now happens occasionally thanks to the new climate which enables people to "come out" sexually after years of repressing their true identity. On the one hand, it is good for them; on the other hand, it can devastate the family they leave behind. As one wife bitterly told me: "If he had gone off with another woman, I could have changed my hairstyle or done other things to try to win him back. How can I compete with another man? I've got no chance."

A relatively recent development has been those who separate late in life, in their seventies or eighties. You would have thought that they had learnt to live with each other by then, got over the battles they used to fight and found compromises. Apparently not, and the opposite can be true. The strain of the quarrels or disagreements, bearable in younger days, becomes too much, and one or both partners decides that they want to end their days in peace. Whereas they feared being alone before, now they welcome it. As one 87-year-old woman told me of her 89-year-old husband, "I have been a good wife for over sixty years, cooked, cleaned, brought up the children and made a home for him; it was never a great match, I've done my duty and now feel I deserve a break." It was impeccable logic and hard to disagree. Still, such late splits can come as a shock to their children (by then in middle age or even approaching retirement), having to visit parents in separate places after a lifetime together; also for grandchildren, who had viewed them as one of the more stable parts of their ever-changing world.

Another trend, though this may be just a coincidence in the families I have come across, is the number of men who have walked out of their marriage when they hit the age of sixty. In all of the four cases I know, there was no other woman (or man) involved and it caught all of the wives totally by surprise. The marriages may have morphed from great passion to steady relationship, but they were not full of screaming rows or silent resentments. I have long felt that sixty is the new forty, whether it be in terms of physical health, mid-life crisis or change in attitude, and this seems to have been the motivating factor. The men had, separately but similarly, all sensed they had reached a milestone, wanted to re-asses their life and felt the need to be free of any ties. All told me that they bore their wife no animosity; it was just that they felt the need to do something different to being married. Naturally, their wives were all devastated, as well as shocked that they had not seen any warning signs. In addition, as they themselves were all approaching sixty and thinking of the retirement they would be sharing together shortly, they felt that their future had been ripped away from them. The result was that, although the men felt no ill-will towards their wives, their wives were extremely angry with them.

Chapter 6

Dispatch

Mourning

My synagogue has a monthly magazine and in each issue I write an "Ask the Rabbi" column, in which members send in a question and I answer it. The questions cover a variety of religious, ethical and ritual matters, but what is striking is that in every year over half the questions will be on the subject of death and mourning rites. It reflects the fact that this is the area that matters most to people, where they are keen to know what to do when, and where they want to do "the right thing by Dad" or "what Mum would have wanted". Perhaps this is because death is such a mystery that the rituals around it become more important than those at all other occasions; or because death takes away loved ones against our will, that doing the designated rituals is a small way of taking back control.

What some may find extraordinary is that although I have taken several hundred funerals, I have only seen a handful (literally) of dead bodies. We do not have any equivalent of the Last Rites in Judaism. There is a final prayer that the person who is dying should say, if they are able to do so, but no role for the rabbi. We do not believe that someone's place in heaven is determined by any last minute repentance or affirmation. This is partly because it should be what happens over their lifetime that judges them, not the last five minutes of it; and partly because there are no set rules for entry into heaven, or even any certainty that there is a heaven in the first place. There is a belief in some sort of afterlife, but it has always been undefined – on the rather practical grounds that no one has ever sent a postcard back to say what it is really like. Instead, Judaism has always urged its adherents to focus on this world, where they can affect what happens, and leave the next world to God. It means, therefore, I am rarely summoned to witness a person's departure. I always visit the family that same day or the next, to support them and to discuss arrangements, but invariably the body has been removed from the house by then, or they have died in hospital or a care home.

There is no doubt that Judaism does a good job when it comes to death. There might be debates over circumcision or queries about the laws of kosher food, but we score well in this area in terms of equality, speed and grief management. Equality is in the fact that there is a strong ethos that you should not be able to tell the difference between a rich person's funeral and that of a poor person. The body is not dressed in any finery, but in a plain linen shroud. The coffin is made of the same cheap and plain wood, be they a millionaire or pauper, without any adornments outside or velvet lining inside. True, you can tell a few things from the car park – whether it is full of gleaming BMWs or battered vehicles – but the service is the same, and we all depart from this world empty-handed, whatever we had the day before. Needless to say, we have little time for the latest marketing ploys, be it multicoloured coffins or ones shaped like a guitar or motorbike. I admit, they can reflect a person's individuality and some designs are very appealing, but there are better ways of saying who that person was and what they stood for. Death is bad enough without adding funereal one-upmanship.

Speed is important too. This dates back to ancient times and especially in hot climates, when, in the absence of mortuaries, a body could deteriorate rapidly and make the room where they lay repugnant. Personally I do not approve of the custom in some Jewish circles of same-day burials. It means that key mourners might not be able to be present, while I think one needs more time for emotional adjustment. People often go through a stage of numbness when first confronted with the death of someone close to them, but holding the funeral immediately sends their feelings into deep freeze. More common is to have the funeral within three days or so. That allows the paperwork to be done less frantically, relatives elsewhere in the country, or even abroad, to arrive and the family to plan the service. However, if the funeral is delayed much longer, there is an awkward period of waiting. There is nothing more to be sorted, so the main mourners are left waiting around, not having the expressive rituals of the funeral or support of those attending, and not wanting to go back to work and normal tasks as if nothing has happened. Time hangs heavy, and although no one looks forward to the funeral, it does help release the wide range of emotions one feels. Perhaps it is cultural conditioning, but whenever funerals have had to be delayed for two or even three weeks – which is the normal length of time arranged for Church ones – it has caused the family deep distress.

What is so distinctive about Jewish funerals is that they are not the final ritual, but only the start of a year-long process. They are followed by a *shivah* (literally "the week") during which time the immediate family stays at home and is visited by friends, neighbours and members of the community. (Immediate family is defined as the seven closest relatives: mother, father, brother, sister, spouse, son and daughter.) People take over food, they chat, they listen, they fill the house with noise and bustle and life. Yes, the family may just want to curl up in a corner alone with their own thoughts, but there is plenty of time at night to do that. Instead, they are forced to tell the story of what happened over and over again, repeat the "if onlys", cry, express exasperation, laugh, get cross and allow all the contradictory, confused and pent-up feelings to pour out. When a non-Jewish neighbour in our road lost her husband, I went to visit her, even though I hardly knew either of them and we were just on nodding terms. She was surprised, but I explained that was the Jewish way of doing things. Apparently, the other neighbours put a card through the door wishing her well and saying they did not want to disturb her at this sad time, but that she should get in touch if there was anything they could do for her. I know she valued my one visit more than their ten cards, while it reinforced for me the value of the *shivah*: there is nothing that beats the warmth of human company.

That first week is followed by the month of mourning, when family members go back to everyday life but with certain limitations, such as not listening to music or attending places of entertainment, be it a cinema or theatre. The idea is to acknowledge in a practical way that the mourner has been hurt and their world disrupted. For the rest of the year, they say the special mourner's prayer, known as *kaddish*, in some circles daily, in others once a week at the Sabbath service. There is also the custom of putting up the headstone on the first anniversary of the person's death (but it can be much earlier) and having a short service at which there is often a large crowd, though some families prefer a more private ceremony. It is a way of both marking the date, but also starting to let go of the grief and turn their gaze forwards. A twenty-four-hour candle is also lit at the home, signifying the life that has existed and then expired. It is also lit at each subsequent year on the anniversary. Thus there is a carefully crafted journey from the funeral to the intense period of the first week to the semi-mourning of the first month, continuing in a measured way throughout the rest of the year, culminating in the stone-setting at the first anniversary, and then with an ongoing annual acknowledgement. It is a gently moving escalator from the depths of grief back into the stream of life.

Personal Choices

So far, I have been careful to refer to funerals, but there are two types – burials and cremations – and they have been the source of much controversy. In the past, Judaism has always opted for burials and fiercely opposed cremation when it first started to be an option in the West. Of course, faith groups for whom cremation is a long and noble tradition are puzzled at such resistance, but such is the power of tradition (which might also be described as "unthinking habit"). In Jewish eyes, cremation was seen as disrespectful – "you burn rubbish, not bodies" – while there was also a theological objection: Orthodox Judaism believes that one day, in the messianic era, bodies will be reunited with their souls and resurrect. If the body has been destroyed in a fiery furnace, the logic goes, then the soul will remain forever homeless. This attitude changed with the arrival of Reform Judaism in 1840, which no longer subscribed to the idea of a physical resurrection and spoke instead of a spiritual afterlife. In addition, it was very obvious that cremations were being conducted with exactly the same decorum as burials. Personally, I would add that even within Orthodox thinking it should be permitted, for once you were in the realm of the miraculous, then anything can happen, and if dead bodies can jump up, then so can dead ashes.

In Reform synagogues, therefore, which includes my own community, cremations have long been permitted and are increasingly common. Personally, I think there is some value for the family having a physical place to visit, sit on a bench and muse to themselves, which is easier to do at a cemetery than a garden of remembrance, but I fully accept that is purely my view and may not apply to others. The key factor is the preference of the person concerned and that they have the right to choose what they wish to happen to their remains. This had led to occasional battles on my part when someone has left written instructions opting for cremation, but a close family member from the Orthodox tradition has demanded a burial instead. Cremation may not be my first choice, but I am adamant that a person's last wishes should be observed. The relatives can choose what happens to them when they die, but have to respect the choice of others. What is a more common scenario, though, is that relatives simply do not know what the deceased had wanted. Sometimes this is because they had never got round to discussing it, but it can also be that the person was very reluctant to talk about death, however far off it might appear to be. There is a primeval superstition amongst many that talking about it brings it closer. It is totally irrational, and they probably know that, but it reflects the fact that death is the great unknown. What will happen as I die? Will it be painful? What will happen after I die? Where will I go? Will I still feel it? Will I still be me? It is probably the case that the only thing our brains cannot comprehend is our own non-existence.

Someone who very much bucked the trend was Henry. When I visited him three weeks before he died of what he knew was a terminal condition, he and his wife were very accepting of what lay ahead. I found both of them talking about it and discussing options for his funeral in an astonishing way. They were like a newly engaged couple planning their honeymoon and excitedly looking at various brochures, except that in Henry's case, it was not holiday brochures but funeral parlour catalogues. They were chatting animatedly about how nice it would be to have a horse and carriage. It was a remarkable conversation. Henry said, "Four horses." "No," she replied, "that's a bit much, let's settle for two." Henry: "Okay, but what about them having black plumes?" Her: "Oh yes, you must have them." Henry: "How about a wicker coffin rather than a normal one?" Her: "Yes, if you want." Henry, flicking over some pages: "Look, they can bring a dove and release it into the air during the ceremony; what do you think? Would that be nice?" It was surreal to behold, but very touching and very healthy. It meant that Henry got exactly the funeral he wanted, while it also helped his wife know that she had done everything she could to make it special for him, giving her a lot of comfort in what was still a very difficult time.

Despite the reticence of many people to talk about their demise, it is so much better for the relatives if they know what the deceased had wanted. It saves a lot of frantic searching for any letters or desperately trying to remember snippets of conversation. It is also helpful emotionally if they can feel they are carrying out what the person had wanted. At a time when they feel bereft and helpless, at least they can have the satisfaction of fulfilling one last task for them. I have therefore had an ongoing campaign to encourage people to add funeral details to their will, or to deposit instructions with me to be placed in the "last wishes" file that I keep for all members of the congregation. It can also be therapeutic for the person concerned, for whereas we like to think we are in charge of our fate, there is usually no way of knowing if our death will be tomorrow or several decades ahead. By setting out what you wish to happen, and how and where, you are at least exerting some certainty over the uncertain.

The file – now rather large – has some special requests, such as the ashes being scattered in the Thames by someone who loves boating there, or in a woodland area where another person frequently walks. In one of the very first funerals I ever took, the woman who died had asked that she be buried in her wedding dress. There were a few raised eyebrows in the family, as this went against the plain linen shroud rule, but I thought it was such an important statement about the key moment in her life that I had no hesitation in permitting it. Anyway, to be honest, I was more impressed that at ninety-four years of age, she was still able to fit in it! I was more unsure over another request that I had in advance, a gentleman who requested that his beloved cricket bat be placed in his coffin. I knew he had played cricket for most of his life, and so this was an important part of his identity, but part of me felt it was somewhat pagan. It reminded me of Egyptian pharaohs being entombed with their chariots, or Vikings being buried with their swords. Surely he did not expect to be using his bat again on a heavenly cricket pitch? Despite my misgivings, I did agree on the grounds that it did no one any harm, while I knew it would give him a lot of pleasure to think that he and his willow would lie silently side by side in eternity.

Placing an item in a coffin is still very rare for adults, but is more common in the case of a child death. Often, it is a teddy bear and it fulfils a double purpose for the grieving parents. It gives them a sense of comfort to visualise their child with it, together, as they were in life. It also serves as their substitute, staying with and looking after the child in a way they cannot, making sure their little one is not alone. I always consent. The area that does trouble me, though, is a new trend in the disposal of cremated ashes. I have no problem with them being scatted in obscure places or cast into the sea. If it is meaningful to the person concerned, then so be it. But increasingly there are requests to divide up the ashes and, for instance, each of the three children to have a third and store them at their respective homes. Somehow, that feels very odd; if it was a burial, they would not cut up the body and each take a leg or an arm home with them to put in their back garden! I am also a little wary of those who keep the ashes of relatives on the mantelpiece in an unsealed jar. I do not smoke, but one of my colleagues who does told me how he was visiting a congregant and they were having a cigarette each. You can probably guess what happened next. Just as he was about to tap some ash into a nearby jar, the person screamed: "DON'T, THAT'S MY DAD IN THERE."

New Trends

The actual nature of the service, be it a burial or cremation, has changed enormously. Whereas once it was only the minster who gave the eulogy, now relatives and friends will often be called upon to speak. It is surprising that this did not happen much earlier, as they invariably know the deceased much better than the officiant, but it was largely because the eulogy was seen as a moment of spiritual comfort, not a chatty canter through their life story. Nowadays, congregants prefer biography to theology. Perhaps it was also because ministers did not trust those giving the address to keep within the bounds of decorum. In the main, this has proved an unwarranted fear; the warm tributes and lovely anecdotes of those who knew the person well have been a great reminder not just of what has been lost, but of the many good years that were shared. What can work best is speakers from different parts of their lives (e.g., a relative, a work colleague and a childhood friend) whose remarks reveal different aspects and show how often we see only the surface of a person and not the whole picture, nor the life lived before we got to know them. Still, I have heard a few speakers who have sounded more like the best man at a wedding, with a string of salacious details that left some mourners guffawing and others fuming. It is certainly good to be able to laugh fondly at a funeral, appreciating particular memories, but some incidents are best left unrevealed.

There are still many families who prefer the rabbi to speak, either because they feel tongue-tied or because they do not trust themselves not to break down in the middle of it. The eulogy is a delicate act: on the one hand it should bring out the best in the life of the deceased, so that his or her memory can be honoured; on the other hand, it should not be so full of undeserved praise that mourners wonder if they have come to the wrong funeral. That means acknowledging the whole person, not just their merits, but doing it in a gentle way. When speaking about one, often grumpy individual who also supported a number of local charities, I said: "He was not always good-tempered, but he could be very generous in other ways." When referring to a lady who was good at alienating people, and hence the small turnout at her funeral, I commented: "Sometimes, it seemed that the word 'stubborn' was invented for her." It is important to be honest in an affectionate way and for those present to feel they recognise the person being eulogised. Ministers always know they have summed up someone well when they see people nodding in agreement at what is being said.

Another revolution has occurred in the choice of music at cremations. Previously it was traditional Jewish compositions, suitably solemn and mournful. Now the music is largely secular, sometimes classical music, but very often pop. The music either reflects key moments in the deceased's life (such as the first song they danced to with their spouse), or a favourite hit, or a song that reflects their philosophy. In the latter category, it is remarkable how many people think of themselves as independent spirits and go for Frank Sinatra's "My Way". Another common request is "Always Look on the Bright Side of Life" from Monty Python's *The Life of Brian*. Others opt for a semi-jocular exit, choosing Led Zeppelin's "Stairway to Heaven". Some may regret the occasionally raucous songs, though I always find it one of the unexpected bonuses of cremations to listen to songs that I used to love, but have not heard for decades. There was one week in which I conducted three funerals, all very sad, but with an amazing playlist, from Klezmer to Abba, including Simon and Garfunkel's "Scarborough Fair", as well as songs by Celine Dion and Toyah Willcox. I felt I had a better selection at the crematorium than on the radio! The changes in both the addition of speakers and the selection of music have happened with Christian funerals too, so it is not just a Jewish experience, but more a democratisation of death. The more the ceremony reflects those who have died, the more the mourners will feel they have honoured them, and the greater comfort they will gain.

There may also be another, less positive reason for choosing radio hits rather than liturgical pieces. Many of those attending a funeral simply do not to know the traditional hymns, as the number of people who go to Church regularly is much lower

85

than before. I have noticed this particularly when arriving at a local crematorium and catching the end of the service taking place before my one. So many times I have heard the vicar asking everyone to join in with the final hymn and then be accompanied by a barely audible sound, or even have to sing solo. Jews do not sing hymns at funerals, so I cannot say how forceful or dire our communal singing would be in comparison, and I am not suggesting our decibel levels would be any better.

There is one aspect of cremations that used to puzzle me and took a while to resolve. We had a number of families in the community who had come to Britain in the late 1930s as refugees from Germany and Austria, finding sanctuary here from the growing threat to Jewish lives. When they began to pass away in the 1980s and 1990s, it was noticeable that every single one opted for a cremation. I was surprised, knowing that so many of their family and friends had ended up in the Nazi crematoria. Surely that was the last thing they wanted to be associated with, albeit in a very different context in Home Counties England. I had expected them to choose to be buried, in contradistinction to what happened in those terrible times. Then it occurred to me that maybe cremation was a form of identification with those who had been murdered, a form of survivor's guilt that meant they wished to now share the same end? Eventually, trying to phrase the question as sensitively as I could, I asked one of those remaining what was the reason for this trend. She laughed at my convoluted delicacy and said, "It's simple, German Jews had the custom of being cremated long before the Nazis arrived. So we are carrying on doing what we always used to do, and aren't going to stop just because of Hitler." I was grateful, both for the answer and for the reminder to consider the simple explanation for any problem before looking for more complicated ones.

A new trend that is just in its infancy, but has been well established in other faiths, is setting a photograph of the deceased within the headstone. I remember being shocked at the first one

I saw, feeling as if I was seeing inside the coffin and intruding by looking them directly in the eye. But I know that habit is everything, and the more they proliferate, the more natural they will feel. Yet they raise the question of which photograph to use? In old age, as they were last seen and best remembered by grandchildren, or in their prime in their thirties, the image they may have had of themselves long afterwards? Even more recent are graves with a QR code on them that, when scanned with the right type of detector, reveals the history of the person buried there. If this catches on, then, like going through a museum with an audio-guide headset on, we will be able to move from grave to grave and listen to the story of an entire community.

I am more uncertain about the value of another development: those who pre-record a voice message or video, of themselves before they die, which is then played at the funeral. For some, it is a cheeky attempt to cheat death and be present at their own goodbye ceremony. Others intend it to be a source of comfort to those present, as well as a chance to deliver some final *bons mots*. My gut instinct is that it is inappropriate. One of the key elements of funeral is accepting that the person has died and that, however painful, we will never hear their voice or see their face again. There is no greater reminder of that than the dull thud of earth shovelled onto the coffin, or the closing of the crematorium curtain, with the coffin disappearing from view. It is a reality that many can find agonisingly hard to come to terms with, but is vital to the grieving process, and so anything that appears to refute that is unhelpful. It delays the process of acceptance, and means that instead the mourners have to do it later, alone, and without the structure of the service and attendees to support them.

A slightly related issue is answerphones. Many a time, I have phoned someone up who lost their husband a month ago, to check on how they are managing, and been surprised to hear his voice telling me they cannot answer right now but to call back later. How do I gently tell the widow I just heard her husband speaking to me? In many cases, they had simply not realised his voice was still on the message, as they never phone themselves. For those who know he died, it can be very eerie to hear him cheerfully greet them, while those who have not heard the news will leave a message for him to call back. The problem is that it can be emotionally difficult for the wife to change the message, feeling as if erasing his voice is killing him again. The same can happen in reverse, when a husband has lost his wife. The only difference is that that some widows prefer to leave the original message on the tape for security reasons, reckoning that it is safer if a stranger calling finds a male voice rather than a female one. Once more, the real issue is how to let go of a partner in a way that, however unwelcome, allows the bereaved person to best adapt to their new situation.

There can be a similar problem when a person decides to leave their body to science and there is no funeral to formally start the mourning process. Of course, a memorial service or gathering can occur, but somehow it feels less gutsy without a coffin present. A variation on this was an elderly member who reckoned that his dilapidated body would not be of much use, whereas examining his brain for deterioration might help with Alzheimer's research, and therefore donated just his head. It was a noble gesture, but left mourners with the less than wholesome image of a headless torso in the coffin. I had fully supported his decision, but always advise people to inform relatives of any such decisions, so that they are already used to the idea in advance and not overcome with shock or anger if they only find out after the death. The same applies to organ donations, though they can often be a source of comfort when there is an unexpected death. When a young man suddenly died, his family's grief was assuaged a little in the knowledge that his organs went to help three separate people. It was one of the only positives they could take from a highly distressing loss. This was one of the reasons I firmly supported the change in procedures in 2020, from having to opt into the system to donate an organ, to permission being assumed and only not the case if one had opted out. Put bluntly, I knew of no otherwise healthy person who would refuse to receive an organ if they unexpectedly needed one, and so there was no justification for them to refuse to give one of theirs if they passed away.

Inscriptions have also changed. Not so long ago, apart from the name and dates of the deceased, there was a standard formula which comprised of a verse from the Bible depending on whether it was a man or woman. Now, quotations might be taken from all other types of literature, be it Shakespeare or modern poetry, though it is more common for mourners to compose their own wording. But how do you sum up a person's life in two or three lines? Sometimes they highlight key characteristics ("He achieved all that he wanted and shared everything he had"); other times they reflect the quality of the relationship ("She was always there for me"). The best are ones that bring a warm smile of recognition. Unfortunately some become battlegrounds between the siblings, who can have very different perceptions. There are also those which later come to be regretted. One young and distraught husband, against my strong advice, inscribed, "I will never love anyone else again". Five years on, after he has remarried, he now understands why I was so opposed to it.

Hiccups

There can be plenty of other types of hiccups, though thankfully I have not experienced them myself, but heard about them from colleagues. Beware of those who die abroad and are ferried home, warned one of them, for airline regulations mean that the person is put in an extra strong and large coffin (to prevent any disease affecting the rest of the cargo in the hold or being brought into the country). Unfortunately, in one such case, the cemetery attendant was not informed and dug the grave standard size, not extra large, and so the coffin would not fit as they attempted to lower it. The mourners had to retire to a distance and wait for half an hour until it was widened and the service could proceed. On another occasion, a relative stood too close to the grave and fell in. What was even worse is that his foot went through the coffin (the penalty of Jewish ones being made of thin wood, not sturdy oak) and as the man was pulled out, the coffin lid came up with him. Note to myself: never let people get near the edge.

More commonly, one of the questions that often arises is whether children should come to a funeral. Attitudes seem to have change markedly over the years in this respect. The feeling used to be that children should not attend as it would be too upsetting and only those in their teens should come. Nowadays, it is common for parents to bring much younger children. In some ways, it is healthy for them to regard death as a sad but natural part of the life cycle, to be familiar with cemeteries and to know that adults can cry. However, I always emphasise two key aspects when discussing it with the family: first, that they should explain to the children in advance what to expect and talk through what will happen when, so that even if they are upset, they are not shocked. The former is normal, the latter is unnecessary. Second, that if the parents are the main mourners, they should ask someone close to them to be on standby to look after the children if they are particularly distressed, being a nuisance or need attention for some other reason. Otherwise it compromises the role of the parents at the funeral, and turns them from mourners to comforters, from the son or daughter of the deceased to the mother or father of the children, and prevents them from grieving properly. However, if parents decide not to bring the children, then it is important that they do not feel excluded or given the message that death is too frightening. Instead, they should be given a positive role, such as being told they are in charge of the house (even though they have an adult looking after them) and should be there to greet people when they come back from the funeral, let them in and take their coats. That way they feel part of the process and included in the loss being faced by the family.

There is also the big question of what to tell children about death, with many parents feeling confused as to what is the best explanation. That is partly because they do not wish to upset them, although most children are much more resilient and matter-of-fact than we appreciate. They see dead birds in the garden or squashed squirrels on the road, and know that life is finite. It is also because parents themselves are unsure about death, and often caught between what they would like to believe (we will one day see our loved ones again) and what they actually reckon (once dead, that is the end of the story). The best answer is to be as truthful as possible and I advise something like: "We don't know what happens when we die. The special thing, which we call the 'spark of life' that made Grandpa the person he was, has gone out, so we put his body away, as it will not move or speak again. We probably won't ever see him again, which is why we are sad and cry and have a special goodbye ceremony. In the meantime, we think about all the things we learned from Grandpa, and what we still do have, and the people around us, and all the lovely things we can do together." I am sure that can be improved upon, but I am equally certain about what parents should not say: "He is in heaven" (which just leads to more questions – Where is heaven? What is it like there? Can I go and visit him? – and gets well-meaning parents into deeper theological complexities). Even worse is "God wanted Grandpa to be with Him" (which leads to yet more problems – Why did God do that? Why won't God give him back? I hate God for taking Grandpa away). Eventually, it all comes back to "I don't know", so it is best to start from there in the first place.

It is important to remember that different people grieve in different ways. There is no right way or wrong way to mourn, and the minister's job is to be helpful, both at the funeral and in the months afterwards. Often people want reassurance that what they are going through is normal, such as coping well one day and being in tears the next. Sometimes, the reverse is true: that they feel guilty because they have not been crying and are continuing with everyday life; they worry that it indicates there is something wrong with them, or that they did not care about the person enough. Grief can be delayed and feelings can be numbed, I explain to them, while tears are not the only way to measure a sense of loss. Two pieces of advice I always give, especially to those who have lost a partner and are now living alone. The first is to accept any invitations to visit friends or neighbours. Even if they do not feel like going, it is good for them to get out of the house and engage socially; there is still plenty of time to be alone later on in the day. It is a mistake to refuse invitations and say you will get together later: they tend be proffered in the first week or two after a death; if they are not taken up, they tend to trail off and not be repeated. What is more, if you accept, and then reciprocate the invite, it establishes an ongoing relationship that can prove enormously beneficial in dealing with two of the major problems that widows and widowers face: structuring time when there is no one to share it with you anymore, and carving out a new social pattern for yourself.

The second suggestion is not to move home immediately, unless there is a pressing reason to do so. Downsizing from a big house or changing area may be a good idea eventually, but not suddenly, otherwise you lose not only your partner but also familiar surroundings, neighbours and shopkeepers. It can be a double bereavement and add to the sense of the dislocation. Much better to move after you have dealt with all the paperwork, seen all those "firsts" go by (birthday, wedding anniversary,

Yom Kippur and Christmas). You will also have recovered your equilibrium more, be stronger and more able to face another upheaval.

Children's funerals are enormously painful, with so many unfulfilled hopes and unrealised years. The pain of parents can be compounded if they feel guilty, even though there may be no reason for them to do so, but it is instinctive to think it is your primary duty to protect your child from harm. I have seen some parents become traumatised by their loss for the rest of their days. Others have mourned deeply and desperately, but eventually re-entered the stream of life, whether having another child or carrying on with their lives. The fact that it only rarely happens is testimony to the enormous advances in medicine, as well as a variety of safety measures we now take for granted, from car seatbelts to fairground regulations. But accidents still occur, as do fatal illnesses, and the deaths can feel even more distressing precisely because we no longer expect them in the way that previous generations did.

The worst funerals, though, can be those involving a suicide. Once again, mourners can feel acutely guilty, berating themselves for not noticing any warning signs, or, if evident, not doing more to prevent the suicide. In so many instances, both are unjustified. Many suicides can be "out of the blue", without any hints that something was troubling them. Those that are premeditated are often planned in advance in maximum secrecy, leaving relatives stunned when they discover the meticulous notes left behind. Even those who are clearly distressed can be beyond any efforts of others around them. They occupy a realm of bleakness and despair that is beyond logic and impervious to help. In one funeral I took for someone who had left a note saying how alone and friendless she felt, it was attended by dozens of her friends and colleagues. It was impossible not to cry out, "if only she had known how liked she was", but she was the one person who could not see it and none of the messages ever pierced the darkness that surrounded her. The actual nature of the suicide can also add to the distress of the mourners. Images of the person hanging from a beam or mangled by a train, whether they be witnessed or reported, are terrible legacies. I was criticised in the media for saying that those who end their life that way are unbelievably selfish, but I stick to that opinion. I appreciate that they are not in the right frame of mind to appreciate the consequences of their death on others, and that they may even feel they are doing everyone a favour by killing themselves. Nevertheless, the manner of doing it can make their death even more difficult to come to terms with by those they knew.

Compared to many other Jewish cemeteries (grey, drab, windswept and often cold), we have a very picturesque one in Maidenhead. It is surround by trees and bushes, mostly evergreens, so it is full of colour and life all year round. Part of me thinks that a dour, chilly graveyard is more in keeping with the atmosphere of the occasion, but on balance I reckon that having a comforting and attractive place to visit is much more helpful for those visiting after the funeral, able to sit on one of the many benches and contemplate the cycle of life and the marvels of nature. There is a rule about headstones being a uniform size, which prevents the one-upmanship that happens at some Jewish cemeteries whereby the stones can look like a row of modern skyscrapers, each slightly taller than the other and trying to outdo the previous one. This has always surprised me, as it seems contrary to Jewish ethics about modesty in funerals. If we are all equal then my stone should not be bigger than yours. It is also part of a larger cemetery for all faiths. Each group has its own section and a path around it – Protestants, Catholics, Muslims, Jews, don't knows – independent, but together. It gives a clear message that we all share the same end and that if we are going to lie peacefully side by side in death, we should coexist peacefully side by side in life.

Not everyone who is buried opts to go there. I have twice been called upon to bury members of the synagogue in a church cemetery. This would be unthinkable in past generations, either because a practising Jew would not dream of being buried right next to the church, or because the local vicar would not want a rabbi conducting the service. The new spirit of interfaith dialogue has overcome the latter objection, while special circumstances accounted for the former. In one case, it was a woman who wanted to be buried next to her Christian husband, who was already interred there. Normally, mixed-faith couples opt for a non-denominational cemetery, so that relatives from both sides of the faith divide can come to neutral territory. Alternatively, they choose cremation and their ashes are scattered by the same faithless rosebush. In this particular case, the husband had been a practising Christian and had died unexpectedly. The Jewish wife went on autopilot, contacted the vicar and arranged the church burial without thinking how it might affect her several years later. Although she never envisaged being buried in a churchyard, she did want to be next to her husband. I took the attitude that, if they had been together in life, why should I stop them being together in eternity? It also meant that the children could visit mum and dad in the same place, rather than miles apart. The other case was more geographical: the couple were both Jewish and lived next door to the churchyard. The wife acquired a plot for him (and eventually herself) the other side of the see-through fence that separated their garden from the church. "This way," she told me, "I can walk over to him every morning and say hello; and then 'goodnight' each evening." It was an irrefutable argument.

I was much more dubious about the person who wanted his mother buried in his back garden. Admittedly, it was a spacious one, attractively laid out, and there was an idyllic secluded spot where her grave would be. "What will happen if you move?" I asked him, "will you dig her up and take her with you?" He assured me he would stay for years to come and the property would remain in the family thereafter. It was a lovely setting and the service went well. Four years later, his financial situation changed and he sold the house. I always caution families against home burials. Assuming that they do not cart their deceased relative around with them if ever they move – it is very hard to get permission for exhumations while it can also be distressing emotionally – there are two other concerns: might they then feel very guilty at leaving mum or dad behind? Might it also make selling the property rather difficult, or lower the asking price? Having a pond or pergola in the garden can be an asset, but a corpse?

On a more general point, I am very aware that not all parents are good parents, and so the mourning at some funerals can be very muted and perfunctory. Thankfully, they are the minority and instead I have been told numerous times by grieving children (albeit adult ones) about what a great childhood they had and asked: how can I ever repay my parents? I have a simple answer: you cannot repay them, but you can honour them best by being as good a parent to your children as they were to you.

Questions of an entirely different kind are now arising over pet funerals. Dogs and cats play an increasingly important role in the emotional lives of owners, especially with more people today living alone or whose families reside further away from each other. Some people reading this will scoff at it, while others will understand totally. It reflects the fact that there are many people whose relationship with their pets is so strong that they treat them as a fully-fledged member of the family. Those pets also end up exerting an enormous influence on the lives of their owners: planning their diary around being back in time to let the dog out, finding a holiday flat that takes animals, or making sure they book not only the plane but also the cattery. Owners certainly talk to their pets freely, and quite often reckon they receive some sort of reply. It means that when a pet dies, it is not just a nuisance, like the washing machine packing up, but instead it is a major blow, and after many years of camaraderie together, they feel a real sense of bereavement. They are hit by many of the emotions that swell up when we lose a person, with tears and pain, while there can also be feelings of guilt if it had to be put down. The majority leave the body to the vet to "look after" (i.e. cremate – euphemisms being as common with pets as they are with adults "kicking the bucket" or "going upstairs"), but they still want some form of acknowledgement. Others opt for a DIY burial in the garden, or a more formal ceremony at a pet cemetery. One of the many innovations in the new Reform prayer book is recognition of our feelings about animals. It includes a prayer on losing a pet, which refers to "the years of loyalty and companionship that we have enjoyed, and all the moments of happiness we have shared".

Chapter 7

Congregants!

The sermonator

One of the strange aspects of a rabbi's life, and this will apply equally to vicars and priests, is that for much of the time, most people do not see us in action. We are visible for the public events, such as services, wedding and funerals, but a large part of our work is pastoral, one-to-one and unseen by everyone else. This can lead to jibes that we only work at weekends and have the rest of the week off, whereas we are usually working flat-out midweek, and then continue over the weekend too. Perhaps that is why it is so often described as a "vocation" – because unless we loved doing what we do (or do not, but still think it is enormously important), then the long hours would be totally unacceptable. After all, when did you last hear about clergy going on strike or working to rule?

Pastoral work covers a wide variety of situations: visiting the sick (be it at their home or in hospital); comforting the bereaved a few weeks after the funeral when everyone else has gone back to their normal life but the person concerned is still adjusting to a harsh new reality; discussing a relationship with someone who feels it is close to collapse; trying to help an individual who has just lost his job (which I cannot do much about) and their self-esteem (where I may be able to help); debating options with a parent who is worried about the direction their children are taking, be they teenagers or in their forties; spending time with those who are finding life difficult in other ways.

People often forget about the need for preparation time: sermons do not just happen, while those who reckon that we get into the pulpit and just wait for the holy spirit to guide us are showing more faith than is realistic. Different rabbis have different techniques – some starting work from Monday onwards, others mulling over ideas midweek until one theme emerges, others devoting Fridays to the sermon – and of course some winging it completely (and periodically getting caught out when inspiration fails or someone recognises the article which they have plagiarised). The subject matter varies too: some speaking only on the weekly reading from the Bible, others tailoring their remarks primarily to a Jewish take on current affairs, and yet others try to weave their way through both with varying degrees of success.

What I have never understood about sermons is the mocking stereotypes about them being the "time to catch forty winks". It seems to me that the sermon is potentially the most interesting part of the service, as it is the only variable part. The rest of the prayers or songs are largely the same, whereas the sermon is what makes one service different from the next. What will it be about? What angle will the preacher take? Will I agree with his/her conclusion? There is so much to anticipate. Still, on the basis of "there's no smoke without a fire", I accept that the experience of too many duff sermons, either haranguing congregants or sending them to sleep, has led to that stereotype. It seems that quite a few ministers have ignored Rule No. 1 of all homiletics classes: "Preaching is like coal mining – if, after a while, you don't hit your target, stop boring." Despite my own interest – which may be a professional view, because I am "in the business" – I have learnt not to quiz people too much. When a visiting national figure and regular churchgoer attended the synagogue for a special event one Sunday and mentioned he had just come from church, I asked him if it had had been a good sermon. "Oh yes," he replied, "the minister preached well this morning." Genuinely interested, I made the mistake of saying "What was it about?" A look of panic crossed his face and he scratched his head. "I'm not quite sure. I do remember enjoying it, but can't think of the theme... erm... no... really can't remember at all." I told him his secret was safe with me and that what counted was the moment itself. I think I believed that.

After forty years in the rabbinate, perhaps it is time to confess one of the few things that terrified me at the start: I was happy writing sermons, and enjoyed delivering them, but worried that after a while I would run out of ideas. I could envisage plenty of topics about which to speak for a year or two, but after that? What would be left to say every week? Somehow, that has never been a great problem. Yes, some weeks may have needed more pondering than others, and, yes, I have returned to certain themes as they re-emerged either in the weekly readings or the world at large (such as medical ethics, charity projects, events in Israel or environmental issues), but I have found there is nothing as unexpected and as intriguing as life itself and the number of topics it throws up.

I must also admit to being somewhat disconcerted by one of my teachers at rabbinic college who told me that most of us only have one sermon within us and we merely spend our lives giving variations on the same theme. "Oh no," I thought, "how dull." To a certain extent, he may have a point and my one sermon could probably be summed up as "fulfil your own potential and be nicer to other people". If so, that reflects my practical understanding of Judaism: it is about making us better people and encouraging us to interact positively with those around us. Someone more theologically minded might have their one sermon characterised as "trust in God and all will be well". I was criticised very heavily over my sermons by one member, who said I did not mention God enough, and they subsequently moved to a more God-centred congregation. Personally, I take the attitude that God is mentioned in every single page of the Prayer Book, and most of the Bible readings, so does not need any extra boost from me. Anyway, I do not like name-dropping.

What does surprise me is how some people remember sermons for years afterwards. I have periodically been told by congregants, "I have never forgotten that sermon years ago you gave about..." or "I always remember what you said concerning..." Although I am chuffed that what I said had made an impact, I am also often left in a quandary: I have long forgotten whatever were the apparently immortal words I uttered and would dearly love to know. Do I ask them to remind me and show how shallow I am, or smile benignly and forever wrack my brains trying to recall those lost pearls of genius?

What I have noticed very strongly is the disparity between what I think is a memorable sermon and what others reckon. Many a time I have confidently delivered what I anticipated would be a stunning oration, but which was received with polite interest. Conversely, there have been an equal number of occasions when a sermon I thought was not compelling enough goes down incredibly well. So much depends on not what I say, but what they hear... or, rather, what are the concerns preoccupying them and which my remarks just so happen to touch upon and resonate. As proof of how we ministers can never tell what effect our words may have, I was surprised to see a congregant in his thirties whose jet-black hair of the previous week had suddenly turned grey. The sudden transformation was impossible to ignore and when I asked if everything was okay, he replied, "It was your sermon, rabbi, telling us to get rid of the pretences in our lives. I had gone grey early, but was ashamed and dyed my hair. Your sermon made me realise it was time to be myself without coverups." Wow, I never had that in mind! Conversely, the worst sermon I ever gave might be the one when a congregant walked out in protest at what I was saying. But I know that I was right and he was wrong, and the passage of time has proved it. (It was back in the 1980s on the danger of AIDS, which he reckoned did not affect Jews.) The best sermon I ever gave? Given the above, it is hard to judge, but in terms of hard evidence there was one occasion when I received a standing ovation. (Just for the record, it is unheard of to applaud a sermon, but congregants will call out *sh'coy'ach* – "well done" – if they think it is reasonably noteworthy.) In my embarrassed modesty, I muttered, "Thank you, but don't do it again," and sadly they have obeyed me ever since.

Back to the stereotype: the most wonderful put-down I heard was of a colleague who shall remain nameless. A congregant of his, who was a regular synagogue-goer and usually always on time, was held up one Saturday morning and came in very late. As he came through the outer door, he asked, "Have I missed the sermon?" and was told, "The sermon is over, but the rabbi is still speaking." But look on it from another angle and consider the plight of the minister. Given the millions of sermons composed over the years, it is hard for most preachers to say anything startlingly new, while the multiple commentaries on current affairs instantly available via television, the papers or the internet also make originality hard. It means that there are three mains options open to us. First, we can communicate religious knowledge to congregants who often know far more about world history than Jewish history, and much more about everyday British life than of Jewish practices. Second, we can be a moral voice at a time when self-interest and short-termism dominates, bring an ethical perspective to the fore and remind how Jewish values should affect our behaviour. Third, we can touch a nerve, articulate aloud the inner feelings that members of the community bring with them, whether it be horror, wonder, frustration or the need for action.

The difficult ones

If I am honest, the really hard job of being a rabbi is not writing sermons, but acting on the sermons I have written. If I tell my congregation to always pursue what is right rather than what is convenient, or to judge people by the best within them, not the worst, then I am somewhat obliged to do the same myself. For instance, on the condition that you keep this totally confidential, I can tell you that I take pride in the fact that I have suggested people to be in key roles and with whom I will have to work closely, yet with whom I profoundly disagree on many issues, but I know their talents mean they will be good for the community at large. It is also the case, though I suspect this applies to most ministers, I spend many more hours with those with whom I have little in common, but whose personal problems mean I need to support them, than those whose company I really enjoy. There was one member in particular who had a remarkable ability to take offence where none was intended and who was constantly falling out with others in the community. For a period of three months I had to chat to her after virtually every service, reassuring her that she was still valued and mopping up the emotional havoc she created. Eventually, another member said, "Do you realise that she is taking up more of your attention than anyone else put together?" It was true and I began to appreciate, as I have had to in other such cases, that some people are human equivalents of black holes; however much time your pour into them, they always require more and can suck you into ever-deeper vortices of neediness. The instinct of every minister is to help those who are failing in life, and we spend enormous personal energy in helping them, as well as seeking all kinds of professional assistance for them, yet sometimes you know there are those who will spend their whole life lurching from one crisis to another whatever you try to do. It becomes obvious at that point that whilst you will still be kind and courteous towards them, you cannot continue to carry them and have to let go.

Another difficult choice is when an individual member, who is fully competent but utterly annoying to others, comes into conflict with the wider community. Whose interests do you put first? Obviously, you try to accommodate both, attempt to persuade the individual to temper their behaviour and encourage others to be more tolerant of him/her. In one person's case, the solution was to find him a niche task where he could reign supreme to his heart's content, but have very little impact on those around him. Mission accomplished! However, there have also been occasions when I have decided that, much as individuals have rights and need to be protected, majorities count too. When it was a case of me either telling someone in a particular group – for example, but not actually the case, the music circle – that they are no longer welcome, or that the group was disintegrating because of him, then I opted for group survival. This has happened periodically over the years, but is always hard because the person concerned has rarely done anything obviously terrible, but just been a difficult presence, glaring, contradicting, speaking loudly and making others uncomfortable enough to stay away. How do you say to someone "people don't like you", without actually saying it? In the handful of cases where this was necessary, it was more a matter of persuading them that the particular group they were in was not right for them and they could be happier elsewhere. I am a firm believer in white lies that enable you to achieve a necessary object without wrecking someone's ego. It is a delicate axe to wield, seeking communal harmony without sinking into communal uniformity, valuing togetherness without suffocating individuality. No wonder some ministers are frazzled by the competing demands and suffer from religious burnout.

If I tell you I love my congregation, do not think I am being soppy or trying to please any of them reading this. It is the same love that I have for my family, which is deeply felt but does not stop me also finding them exasperating or downright impossible at times. Thus although much of my communal work is full of positive interactions, it can also involve mopping up spilt milk. In some cases it is a matter of stopping people needlessly harming themselves or their loved ones. I did manage to stop a husband telling his wife about an affair that was long over and would almost certainly never come to light, but which would hurt her immensely and achieve nothing. Truth is important, but some truths are best kept to oneself. This was highlighted by a confession I was unable to prevent: a man in his eighties who was dying and told his son about parts of his life he had never discussed, including two affairs he had several decades earlier. He may have felt better for revealing his secrets, but his son was appalled: it totally changed his view of his father and also meant that his grief at his loss a few days later was hopelessly confused with anger at his father's betrayal of his mother. Equally apoplectic was the wife of a congregant who died suddenly in his fifties. Her sense of grief was halted when, clearing up his papers, she came across a draw full of condoms and a list of the women he had slept with, along with notes assessing his experience with each of them. Moral: if you are going to go astray, do not leave a detailed record.

On a lighter note, I was told of a couple who were both on their second marriage. She had never told her new husband that her hair was dyed blonde and, for some reason, was keen for him not to discover that. One morning she was having her regular hair dye at home when her hairdresser felt unwell and promised to return in the afternoon. Shortly after she came back, the husband came home from work unexpectedly early, so the two of them rushed upstairs and locked themselves in the bathroom. He thought she was in there with another man and he had caught them red-handed. He banged on the door and demanded they come out. The hairdresser called out that she was doing the wife's hair and they would not unlock the door till they had finished. This led him to then think they were both in there naked and having a lesbian tryst. He kept on banging until they both emerged and told him the terrible truth. A comedy of errors or a lesson in communication?

The same verdict could be given about an elderly member who I liked enormously, but who "had his moments". He was driving to a hotel in the countryside, to which he had not been before. He got lost and so used his car phone on loudspeaker to call them for directions. Whilst talking to the receptionist, a woman driver swerved in front of him. "You stupid cow," he yelled at her. "I beg your pardon, sir," said the receptionist, thinking he was speaking to her. "No, not you, you stupid cow," he replied, "I meant the other stupid cow." Some rabbis do have them.

Still, I have been spared a fate that many colleagues feel they are duty bound to endure: lunches and dinners following a bar/batmitzvah or wedding. It became apparent in my first year or two as a rabbi that when I was invited to such functions, I was often given the role of sitting next to the impossible aunt that no one else could bear, or opposite the lovely cousin who had halitosis and they reckoned I would be more tolerant of him than others. I quickly decided this was not my favourite occupation. Just as importantly, I reckoned I could use more constructively the four or five hours such functions took and instead do two or three congregational visits in the same time. I therefore attend the reception, greet friends and relatives of the family and then head on my way. It also means I have missed hundreds of speeches, some of which I know would have been both moving or amusing, though others of which would have been dull or excruciating. I can still recall some distinctive ones from those very early years, such as the Belgian relative of a groom whose surname was Cont. The relative gave a very warm speech about the newly-wed couple, but could not understand the suppressed mirth of the guests when he said he hoped that they would have "lots of little Conts"; thinking they had not heard properly, he repeated it again. Then there was the father of the batmitzvah girl, who not only praised his daughter's talents, but paid tribute to his wife and her many qualities. He ended by saying, "Of course, more sex would be nice." I think most of those present have long forgotten what the girl did, but still recall that remark forty years on.

I must confess to having an encounter with a naked congregant, although it is not as dramatic as it sounds. She was an extremely beautiful lady and her husband was an artist. He had painted a nude portrait of her, which a friend living in London had bought and had in his office. It just so happened that, without realising the connection, I went to see the friend on a business matter, and I saw the painting. When I next met the lady in synagogue, I almost quipped: "I nearly didn't recognise you with your clothes on, but held back lest those standing next to her might take it the wrong way.

Disparate tales (but all true)

We have several American families in the community who have come to this area for three or five-year contracts owing to the number of international software companies based locally. They are used to new neighbours throwing a barbecue welcome for them, not British reserve, with brief "hello, how are you?" and not waiting for a reply. I try to explain that underneath we are friendly, and that the best way to meet people locally is to get a dog. When out walking, people will talk to it, eventually see a lead, then notice a hand at the top of the lead, and then work their way up to you. The same applies to a pram or buggy, with locals cooing over the child and eventually getting round to acknowledging the person pushing it.

I have been very pleased to be able to say that although one of my duties for many years was to be a visiting chaplain to Reading Gaol, none of the Jewish inmates I saw were members of my synagogue. They had largely been offenders from elsewhere who had been caught and sentenced locally, or were those picked up by the police at Heathrow Airport. Still, I have had to appear in court for one or two members to give character references when they had committed minor misdemeanours. One case was a woman who had been shoplifting, even though she came from a relatively prosperous home. It was a classic case of a cry for help from someone in a difficult marriage. Another case was more serious, with a woman who had a husband, children and job pushing the self-destruct button and losing all of them through her actions. In the end, although she was arrested before she could commit her intended crime, I still feel angry not only at what she nearly did, but the way she hurt everyone around her.

For another congregant, their story was of a joke that turned into a nightmare. There is the well-worn story of two low-life men who meet up in a pub. One says: "I was sorry to hear your business burnt down last night." The other replies: "Shh – it's tomorrow." Andy (not his actual name) had a factory that burnt down. The loss adjusters reckoned it was not an accident but the result of arson. But who did it? It was in the days before CCTV was ubiquitous and no culprit had been spotted. When they looked at the company's books, they found a massive deficit and accused Andy of causing the fire himself so as to claim the insurance and recoup his losses. Andy protested his innocence and had to endure a lengthy police investigation with the threat of prison hanging over him for two years. Eventually, it was decided not to proceed with any charges and the insurance cover was awarded. But by that time, the business had collapsed and his health had taken a huge toll. Whilst he eventually regained his life and started up a much smaller business, there was always one particular joke we were careful never to tell in his presence.

One of the most precious things we clergy can give people is time. So often other people either do not have the resources, or do not sense the need, to listen to someone pouring out their deepest feelings. Doctors do not have the time, counsellors do but charge, and relatives get fed up. It can be a sensitive matter, knowing when to just listen, when to probe with questions and when to stop them being self-indulgent or sidetracked and move on. Occasionally, though, we can be led down the garden path.

I was at a wedding and found myself standing next to a friend of the groom. I asked him if he was married or still carefree, upon which he launched into a fifteen-minute monologue about his long-term girlfriend of seven years. Apparently, family and friends were pressurising them to name the date and he was resisting. Eventually, I interjected and asked him why he was so hesitant? Was he unsure as to whether he loved her, or maybe he was frightened of commitment, or worried that it would change the relationship? He continued agonising on his dilemma for another ten minutes, and then suddenly said: "Can I tell you a secret? – but you must keep it to yourself." I agreed, whereupon he said, "Actually we got married six months ago in a simple registry office ceremony, but nobody knows." I wanted to wallop him round the head and scream, "So you have already made the decision. Why on earth where you wasting my time telling me you were not sure whether to go ahead or not?" I resisted the temptation, and instead asked why he was worrying so much, and why, having made the decision, he did not tell others. But at that point someone else joined us, the conversation changed and he went off, though it is fairer to say he slunk off. I was left mystified, sworn to secrecy and mourning the half an hour by which my life had been shortened.

There are other times when I am immensely proud of my members. Rod (real name when it is good news!) lived very near to a shop that was sold to a Muslim butcher, who would be using it to sell halal meat. Shortly after that became known, a local racist put up some pig's trotters on the door. Rod took them down, replaced them with a bunch of flowers and a hand-written note that said: *Shalom*/welcome. Good on you, Rod.

Sometimes, I know that whatever I do will end up badly. I was staying with friends in a small flat and not only did the bedrooms have thin walls, but they were exceedingly noisy when making love. I knew that after I left, her father was coming to stay with them for a while, having recently lost his wife and wanting some support. I had met him before and knew he was both old-fashioned and highly emotional. He would certainly find the noise very distressing. Should I warn my friends about their high sexual decibel level? Would they be terribly offended to know I had inadvertently heard every grunt and groan, or be grateful that I had saved them from accidentally upsetting her father when he was in such a vulnerable state? Whose embarrassment was more at stake, theirs or mine? In the end, I decided to tell them. They thanked me politely, but after I left, they never spoke to me again. I hope that at least the father slept well at my expense.

Another lesson in good intentions going astray occurred when on holiday in the Scottish highlands one Christmas. I was walking across some fields by myself when I heard a dog whimpering. His paw had been caught in a serrated metal clamp that was (illegally) designed to trap deer. I went over to him, managed to force the clamp open to release him and off he ran. First, however, he bit me. Thanks a lot! It also meant finding a doctor to give me a tetanus jab, who was not pleased to be disturbed over the holiday period and told me off for messing around with animals. Hopefully you will be more sympathetic than the dog or doctor was.

By far the most embarrassing occurrence was much nearer home, literally only a few roads away from where I lived. I made a visit to Jack White, whom I had not seen for some months and wanted to check on. He was a stocky man, with thick-set eyes and always immaculately dressed. I rang the doorbell, but there was no answer. I was about to leave when the door was opened by a strange looking man whom I had never seen before, rake thin, bulging eyes, wearing just a white T-shirt, a nappy and no trousers, with his tongue rolling in and out of his mouth. To say he looked not only dishevelled, but maniacal was an understatement. I wondered if he was an intruder and Jack was lying on the floor in one of the rooms with a head wound. I said

I had come to see Jack White. He replied: "I am Jack White," which fuelled my fears about him being a villainous impostor even further. I said, as politely as possible: "No you're not. Is Jack White in?" He: repeated: "I'm Jack White." This time I was more emphatic: "No, I know Jack White and you are not him; where is he?" wondering whether I should push past him to see if a blood-stained body was round the corner or run off and call the police. The man became very agitated and in a voice high pitched with insistence, screamed: "I AM JACK WHITE." I looked more closely at the ragged figure and began to see a distant likeness to Jack and realised it was indeed him. I stammered an apology: "I am so sorry, I didn't recognise you. I hadn't heard from you for a while and thought I'd come round to see if maybe you were ill." In a voice still high pitched with a mix of exasperation at my ineptitude and relief that he was at last being recognised, he responded: "I AM ILL!" It turned out he had developed a particularly unpleasant form of cancer, which had ravaged his once fine body. My satisfaction that my intuition had been right was vastly outweighed by my shame at the distress I had caused by denying who he was. It must be awful to be told you are not the person you know you are.

One of the external involvements I have had is being on the Council of St George's House, the forum at Windsor Castle for confidential Consultations between leaders in the field of agriculture, the arts, religion, science and many other aspects of national life. It was established by Prince Philip as a vehicle for them to think "outside the box" away from the public gaze and often with other protagonists whom they might not otherwise meet. Apart from being a fascinating role, it also meant regular meetings with him over the years. At the risk of being hauled off to the dungeons next time I go to the Castle, I can say that he is in private exactly as he is in public, with a mix of total dedication to national causes and a robust way of expressing his thoughts. I recall one discussion over prison reform and another Council member saying we needed to encourage better conditions so as to make inmates more comfortable during their stay. "Nonsense," his Royal Highness responded, "we need to make prison so unpleasant that people don't want to risk going back inside again." I guess that would be labelled "the deterrent approach".

The Prince has an instinctive preference for directness that makes him much more interesting than listening to politicians mouthing platitudes or engaging in verbal gymnastics. Moreover, one person's gaffe is another person's truth. One instance I read about in the press, but did not witness myself, is that when visiting a school and asking a child what he wanted to be when he grows up, the child replied, "A space explorer." The Prince is supposed to have riposted, "But you are too fat to be an astronaut." Quite apart from how accurately that was reported, was that a brutal blow to the child's ego that blighted the rest of his schooldays, or a helpful piece of advice that altered his lifestyle and improved his future prospects? Prince Philip was equally capable of challenging the high and mighty. When discussing the plight of England's uplands, for instance, which had become depopulated in recent years, a leading expert started pontificating imperiously on how important it was to get ordinary people to settle there. "Why talk about it?" replied the Prince, "If you want people to do that, go there yourself and get people to follow your lead." The man fell silent.

For clergy of all faiths, talking about morality is our stock trade, be it in public sermons or private conversations; but are there some moral exemptions that apply to us? One example might be overtaking hearses. I have always thought it bad form to do so. A hearse is not just another car, but quintessentially different. Somehow it feels rude to rush past, as I should not be in such a hurry for my next appointment when an individual has recently left this life forever. Nor should I worry about a few minutes delay when the surviving partner's whole world has just collapsed. So what is the exemption? When I am supposed to be at the funeral grounds to greet the hearse and the mourners on their arrival at the cemetery! I think a dispensation is justified on such occasions, though it does mean ducking as I whizz past. I know one colleague who had the reverse experience: he was driving towards the cemetery in good time, when a full-laden hearse overtook him at 70 mph – which he reckoned was a bad case of religious one-upmanship.

A Rabbi's Charter?

Reflecting on both what a great job being a rabbi is, and the hiccups and pitfalls involved, I wonder whether we should have a rabbi's charter, or clergy charter in general, just as some other professional bodies do. It could include both our duties, but also our protections. It might read as follows:

1. Services should be conducted in a way that is inclusive and makes everyone present feel involved and uplifted.
2. There should always be a short sermon that has been carefully prepared, is intelligible and gives worshippers a thought to take away with them and mull over afterwards.
3. Everyone present should be acknowledged, be it through a smile, nod, handshake or remark.
4. Newcomers should never be left standing alone, but introduced to other members.
5. The minster should be available to discuss a wide range of pastoral issues, be willing to help where possible and able to refer on where not.
6. All requests for help should be responded to within a day, even if an actual meeting is not held till later.
7. Weddings, funerals and other cycle of life ceremonies should not be in "factory line" mode, but tailored to the individual or family concerned as much as possible.
8. The minister has the right to make decisions, including

controversial ones, based on his/her training and religious authority, but should consult first so that they are based on understanding different concerns.

9. Ministers need to be aware that they cannot demand respect; they have to earn it.

(10. I have avoided the temptation to find a tenth so as to parallel another collection of rules – in this context, nine is enough!)

Conversely

1. Ministers should be on a salary that reflects their training and workload.

2. They should be provided with the support necessary to fulfil the job expectations, such as an office, secretarial assistance, use of a car and travel expenses.

3. In-service training should be available, as well as a sabbatical break, to help recharge batteries given the fact that they are rarely off duty

4. Ministers are there to serve, but should not be treated as servants. They should be viewed as professionals and approached in the same way.

5. The minister's partner and children should be treated as people in their own right, not as job add-ons.

Chapter 8

Wider Society

Other faiths

Up to this point, I have often used the word "minister" as interchangeable with rabbi, not just for the sake of variation, but because our working life is so similar. However, it is only right to point out that there are some key differences. A key one, for me at least, is that I think it is much easier for me to promote my faith than many vicars find promoting theirs. As I intimated earlier in the book, Christianity seems to have one main selling point – faith in Jesus – and if you do not buy into that, all the other good things it has to offer are obtainable elsewhere. Judaism may be God-based, but it is not God-centred, and for those for whom this holds little value, I have various other attractions in my sales kit. These include communal camaraderie, moral code, family involvement, sense of history, social action, personal meaning and cultural activities. They are certainly not unique to us, but you can have them God-free and when so many people either do not believe or are unsure as to what they believe, this is a big advantage. Architecture gives the game away. Step into most churches and it is a place of worship, maybe with an activity hall that was built later and tacked on. Enter a synagogue and it is a communal building where the first things you see are the loos and a noticeboard telling you about the mothers & toddlers group, bridge club and sponsored bike ride. Again, not unique to Judaism, except that the likelihood is that, unlike church, most of those involved will not be seen at services, nor even think that they should be attending them.

At the risk of being told I am wrong, though I am happy for anyone who wants to correct me to do so, I think I would also feel very depressed if I was a vicar right now. Jews are used to being in a minority and have had almost two thousand years' worth of conditioning. For Christians, used to being the majority and to dominating the life of the country for centuries, it must be very galling to see the tide of faith receding so markedly. We never claimed to be the one and true faith, so do not have much to lose by not being that. Yes, we are supposed to be "a light to the nations" (Isaiah 42.6), but not the controlling power. If a synagogue closes, it is usually because of demography, because congregants have moved to a new part of the town or out of the area completely. If a church closes, it is because of irrelevance, because the public at large has decided it is no longer meaningful to them. I say this without any satisfaction, for I know how hard vicars work to keep congregations going, while it is sad to see magnificent buildings, once so full, go to waste. Like the tin mines and coalmines that have disappeared throughout the country and that were once so important to our national life, churches are on the retreat too. I am sure that, unlike those mines, many will remain (and some still flourish), but I am struck by the number of Christian clergy who tell me, "You are not the only minority faith, we are too." It is always said with a mix of genuine warmth and deep sadness.

This highlights one of the great revolutions in religious life: interfaith dialogue. For centuries, Jews and Christians have been enemies, rivals, antagonists, opponents and many other negative terms. This was due to a toxic mix of religious and social reasons that, certainly in England, have largely been put behind us. At rabbinic college, and most Christian training seminaries too, interfaith relations are now part of the curriculum. When I first came to my congregation in Maidenhead, it was taken for granted that I introduce myself to the local vicar. Over time, this has now been extended to the local imam and the leaders of other faith groups in the vicinity.

This is a truly wonderful – and very religious – development, and although it is very much the norm, it still needs appreciating.

What is particularly important is that it operates on two separate levels, involving both laity and clergy. The links between the latter mean that similarities and differences can be discussed on a theological level, while the contact between ordinary members means that it has a social impact too, building bridges where barriers previously existed. As is still often pointed out in a voice of pleasant surprise, members of different faiths discover they have much more in common with each other than they imagined. They also come to realise that religious differences can be much less significant than religious indifference.

For clergy, there is a special bonus in that rabbis, vicars and imams find they can discuss the G-word with each other much better than they can with the congregants. We share a similar vocabulary, do not mind asking awkward questions and are happy to challenge assumptions. Compared to some conversations with congregants, it feels like the difference between swimming freely in the sea rather than constricted to lanes in a pool. Of course, there are limitations too, but they tend to be more to do with approach than with faith itself. I have often noticed at interfaith gatherings that after the formalities have finished and the socialising starts, people do not divide up according to their respective faith, but into two groups: liberal Jews, Christians and Muslims being one, and orthodox Jews, Christians and Muslims being the other. Each group sees both their faith and the world at large through a similar lens. It is often the case that, for instance, a liberal Jew can relate more to a liberal Christian than to an orthodox Jew. That may not apply to all areas, but it does to many.

Interfaith dialogue has also had a side advantage in accidentally facilitating intrafaith dialogue. For many years, for instance, Orthodox rabbis would not be seen in public with Reform rabbis. It was seen as endorsing a heretical sect. However, the "cover" of meeting Christian or Muslim clergy meant they could be in the same room and, lo and behold, talk to each other even though they would not do so in other contexts. The same applies to divisions within other faiths. It is a supreme irony, for example, that the Council of Christians and Jews (CCJ) has done as much to heal internal Jewish wounds as it has done for the Jewish-Christian divide. It highlights the uncomfortable fact that religion can be the inspiration for many achievements, but also the source of much friction. We modern clergy look back on aspects of the religious past with horror and desperately try to shift the balance sheet to a more positive outcome today.

I do have mixed feelings, though, about one feature of our inter-religious cosiness. It is good that we meet, great that we learn about different traditions and tremendous that we understand each other better. But at what point does admiring someone else's rituals or beliefs lead to envying them and reckoning that it is a shame we do not have something similar? Conversely, at what point does thinking that someone else's rituals or beliefs are bizarre lead to wondering whether ours appear equally ridiculous, or may even be so in reality? There are very few instances of interfaith dialogue leading to someone converting from one religion to another, while any attempts to do so by those involved are strictly against the rules of engagement. But I suspect, that such dialogue does lessen certainty and conviction. How can you continue to think that you adhere to the best possible faith when you meet so many intelligent and caring people in another one? Of course, the familiarity of our own tradition, along with the personal sense of belonging within our own community, means that we stay rooted in them, but perhaps less convinced than before. It is still where we feel religiously comfortable, but we gradually switch from thinking we have "the true faith" to "a faith with truth in it". Maybe this is good, and it is far healthier if we question more and assert less. However, it can also open up a divide back in our own community between those who operate solely within it and those who interact with others outside it.

The former can regard the latter as being needlessly distracted, while the latter can view the former as being too rigid. Much depends on whether it is thought better religiously to question and explore, or to affirm and proclaim. What is not in doubt is that religious dialogue forces everyone involved to look in the mirror and see not our reflection, but how we appear in the eyes of other people.

If I frequently compare rabbis to vicars, it is because we not only lead parallel lives, but share such strong roots in the Old Testament. Of course, we Jews do not call it that, because for us it is the only testament and saying "Old Testament" could be taken as a value judgement. If you have two raincoats, for instance, then you call one the "new" and the other the "old", but if you only have one raincoat, then it is the "raincoat". The term we generally prefer (apart from the Hebrew term *tanakh*) is the "Hebrew Bible", which neatly distinguishes our bit from the later Greek addition. Personally, I do not fret too much over these matters and, in the same vein, have never felt shy of using the initials BC and AD, even though they are heavily Christological. For me, they were just linguistic conventions that ensured we could communicate. I have been intrigued at how the introduction of more politically correct – i.e. neutral – abbreviations, BCE (Before the Common Era) and CE (Common Era) seem to have caught on so fast. It reflects two factors: first is the general trend towards language that is more inclusive. This has been especially welcome in the prayer book, such as changing references to "the God of our fathers" to "the God of our ancestors", or altering "all men shall praise You" to "all people shall praise You". It applies also to descriptions of God, who is no longer "King of the universe" but "Sovereign". There were howls of protest by some at this development, who were often the same people who had fulminated at the change from "thee and thou" to "you" a few decades earlier. They seemed to forget that the Bible and Prayer Book were first written in the idiom of their time and designed to speak to people immersed in everyday life and language.

The second factor is the change within the religious landscape of British society, which was once primarily Christian with a small Jewish minority, to one that is multifaith, which now includes large numbers of Muslims, Hindus and Sikhs, not to mention Buddhists, Jains, Rastafarians and others. In religious terms, Britain has leapt from monochrome to rainbow coloured within fifty years. This has had an impact on rabbinic life too. Having got used to regular contact with Christian clergy – despite reservations in some quarters (that proved groundless) that dialogue was a sneaky attempt at converting us – we now had to extend that to others. This was by no means a simple exercise. One issue was time. Suddenly, there was an avalanche of interfaith groups that were being formed – bilateral or across the board – and while each was most welcome, they meant stretching a busy diary even further. Another issue was inclination. There was a common heritage with Christians, but the same did not apply to most other faiths. So whilst it was still very enriching to learn about them, and to explain Judaism to them, the sense of kindred roots was lacking. There was also a problem with the one faith that did have such links, Islam, owing to the hostility between so many Muslim countries and Israel. It has been one of the great religious achievements in recent years that we have been able to rise above the political tensions and create a calm atmosphere in which to explore the religious themes of both faiths. As a generalisation, British Jews and Muslims may have strongly differing views about the rights and wrongs of what is happening in the Middle East, but we have been determined not to import the bad relations over there into our own backyard here. It was very pleasing, therefore, that when the mosque in Maidenhead was undergoing building renovations which overran the completion date and they were unable to hold a major event that had been planned, the imam called me to ask if it could be transferred to the synagogue building. It was not just that he had my name and telephone number in his diary, but that he had no problem in holding a Muslim event in a Jewish building. Nor did I, and it went ahead on the due date.

What is fascinating about interfaith dialogue today is how much it has evolved. Originally, the mere fact of a rabbi and vicar meeting was revolutionary; then it was extended to our respective flocks; at first, the meetings themselves were geared to a "feel-good" outcome, looking at how much we had in common or what we could learn from areas in which we differed. Now we have reached a level of sufficient respect and trust to look at the difficult areas where we clash or our scriptures say unpleasant things about each other. This applies especially to the New Testament and passages which not only malign Jews in the time of Jesus, but were taken by later tradition to denigrate Jews throughout the ages. A classic example is when the Jews in Jerusalem are purported to have said "His blood be upon us and upon our children" (Matthew 27.25). This was interpreted by the Church fathers to mean that Jews of subsequent generations were just as guilty of the death of Jesus as those first-century ones. Of all the crimes one can commit, deicide has to be one of the worst, and so it led inexorably to the depiction of Jews as evil and deserving persecution. Descriptions of the Pharisees as dogmatic, uncaring and "a generation of vipers" (Matthew 3.7) may not seem so bad until one realises that the Pharisees was the name for the rabbis of old and some of the most venerated Jewish religious teachers. They include Hillel, Akiba and Judah the Prince. It is certainly true that Christian leaders today have totally repudiated the idea of inherited guilt, while they also see Jesus as stemming from a Pharisaic tradition. The problem is that while such declarations are very welcome, most people still read the bare text of the Gospels but never see the reinterpretations. Thus they still imbibe the anti-Jewish rhetoric, and the cycle of religious prejudice continues.

There are some unpleasant references to Jews in the Koran too, such as the repeated line that "Allah has cursed them [the Jews] on account of their unbelief" (2.88; 4.46) or the description of Jews as monkeys and swine (5.60). Modern Islamic scholars have tried to lessen their significance, but the verses can still have a negative impact on readers. Just for the record, there are also some passages in the Hebrew Bible that rabbis would now deem unacceptable. The classic one is the verse in Exodus 21.24: "An eye for an eye, a tooth for a tooth", which advocates direct physical retribution when one person harms another. The fact that the rabbis effectively annulled it way back in the first century by saying it meant "An eye's *worth* for an eye, a tooth's *worth* for a tooth" and entailed fiscal compensation for the injury (for the pain, lost income, public embarrassment and medical costs) is irrelevant to many who simply read the original text and see it as proof of Judaism's vengeful nature and harsh legalism.

There is one solution, but I suspect it is impossible to implement: change our sacred texts. Re-word the originals so that those buying a Bible are not misled into religious bigotry or have to unlearn what they read. If the Highway Code contains driving instructions that we now think are counterproductive, they will be altered, a new edition produced and learners will only be given the new version. Why can the same not be done with religious codes? I appreciate that, however logical, this is not going to happen, as very few will wish to alter revered writings. A second suggestion would be to put any potentially offensive passages in smaller print, or in a different colour, so as to alert readers that these verses need to be treated carefully or are subject to re-evaluation. It would require tacit admission that some passages are less sacrosanct than others –but is not humility supposed to be a religious virtue?

For any vicars still smarting at the thought above that they can be perceived as being other-worldly and not fully engaged with the gory realities of everyday life, as I know most of them are, I shall share a wonderful story told by a heroic colleague of mine, the Revd. Dr Simon Woodman, minister of Bloomsbury Central Baptist Church. He was at a Baptist Conference, talking in a discussion group about the afterlife and mentioned that he was not sure if he believed in it as an actual reality and was wrestling with what exactly it meant. A fellow minister turned round to him and said, "You know what your problem is? You don't have enough faith" (so much for listening to honest reflection and genuine debate). Later that evening, Simon saw him at the bar, went over to him and said: "I was very upset by your remark earlier today, so much so that I feel like hitting you right now and breaking your nose; but if you have faith that you can pray to God to heal you immediately, then I'll feel good about having hit you and you won't suffer any long-term consequences. So how about it?" The man apologised. A brilliant example of robust Christianity!

But to end this theme on a positive note, a story I often share when giving talks to interfaith groups is about a rabbi and his two friends, a vicar and a Catholic priest. They lived in the same town in the USA and used to meet to play poker once a week for small stakes. The problem was that it was a very conservative town and gambling was banned, so they had to do it privately. One night, as they were playing, the local sheriff burst in, caught them red-handed and hauled them off to the judge. He listened to the sheriff's evidence, looks at the priest and sternly demands: "Were you gambling?" The priest looks heavenwards, whispers "Forgive me Lord" and says "No, of course not." So the judge turns to the vicar: "Were you gambling?" The vicar crosses his fingers behind his back and says "No." So the judge asks the rabbi: "Were you gambling?"

The rabbi replies: "With whom?" I like the story because it highlights how not only are they firm friends regularly spending

leisure time with each other, but they're all equally innocent...
or guilty. They know that their fate is bound up with each other;
they stand or fall together. Like us, they are now irrevocably
intertwined in this multifaith, multirace, multicultural society
of ours. The only sadness is that there are still plenty of parts
of the world where telling such stories, or ones involving other
faiths, would result not in shared laughter, but cries of heresy
and death threats.

Schools

If interfaith work takes up time, this applies even more so to
local schools. I know this is part of the "bread and butter" tasks
of all clergy, but I was the first full-time rabbi in Maidenhead, so
there had been no one before to address school assemblies, talk
about Judaism in the RE lessons or discuss religious themes with
the GCSE or A level students. On top of this, the membership of
the synagogue covered not just the town itself but was scattered
throughout Berkshire, Buckinghamshire, Oxfordshire and some
of the adjoining counties too. If you tot up the number of schools
in that catchment area, it meant that I was in constant demand.
Eventually, doing school visits threatened to become a full-
time job and so we established a team of helpers to share the
load. I quickly learned not to assume any religious knowledge
among the pupils, even amongst Church of England schools.
With a few notable exceptions, I was constantly surprised by the
levels of religious illiteracy. Not only did most children have no
knowledge of Judaism – okay, why should they, that was why
I was there – but very little of their own, Christianity. Having
gone to schools which either had a Christian base (Orley Farm
School in Harrow) or that were religion-free but still treated it
as a matter of general knowledge (University College School
in Hampstead), I was taken aback at how many children were
either "lapsed C of E" or "nothings". Forty years on, there are
many who are also the children or grandchildren of "nothings"

and have no knowledge of even the Bible.

Once again, if I was a vicar, I would find it hard not to despair at what had gone wrong and why the country had departed so profoundly from its Christian roots. As a rabbi, I still regret their ignorance, because it makes religious tolerance much harder to promote. If you do not understand and value your own faith, you are less likely to understand and value that of someone else. It also meant I was unable to make connections: if the children had never heard of the Last Supper, there was no point telling them it was based on a Passover meal. I also had to be careful of inadvertently bringing Judaism into disrepute through the box of items that I brought along to show them. A *tallit* (prayer shawl) or the eight-branched candelabra that was lit at the festival of *Hanukkah* were fine, but just as I was about to take out the *tefillin* (prayer boxes), I realised that telling 13-year-olds that some Jews put leather straps on every morning might sound too much like a sexual fetish and jettison any credibility for the rest of my talk. Anyway, there was a much more important fight on my hands, which was to combat the image of Jews in the textbooks most of them were using. Understandably but wrongly, they wanted to create memorable images, as well as highlight the differences between the faiths, and so always depicted us as ultra-Orthodox, with long black beards, black hats and coats. That is certainly true of some Jews, but by no means all, in fact only of a small minority. Arriving in an ordinary jacket and tie and looking "normal" was the first lesson. The best moments were when I came into the classroom before the children and sat in the corner, they trooped in, did not pay much attention to me and then, when the teacher said, "I am very pleased to welcome the rabbi," they looked puzzled and said, "Where is he?" Bingo!

I also wanted to correct some of the terminology used in their books. To me, "skullcaps" is not only a very old-fashioned word, but conjures up the image of something on a skeleton. I did not expect them to remember the Hebrew word *kippah*, but I was keen that they knew we wore a "head covering" when in synagogue. Their own language could vary markedly depending on their social reference points. When I showed children in local comprehensives a *shofar*, the ram's horn blown at the Jewish New Year, they said, "Ah, it's like a trumpet"; when I showed the same object to the boys at Eton, they exclaimed "Ah, it's a hunting horn." Still, for those who were brought up in an era when RE classes simply meant studying the New Testament, it is worth celebrating the fact that most schools now see it as an opportunity for multifaith studies. Children should certainly be grounded in Christianity so as to understand the history and culture of the country, but knowing about the faiths of many others now living in Britain is important as a matter of both general knowledge and social cohesion. I remember sharing a taxi with an MP when we were en route from Liverpool station to a political conference at which I was speaking. He told me that he went to a Catholic school as a child several decades ago, and they had covered other faiths, but that it had been in the Heresy Class!

A question that some children ask is: was I born in Israel? The answer is "no, I was born in London and have lived in England all my life." But behind the question is the more complex one of what is the relationship between British Jews and Israel. Obviously, there is a special link, partly because that is where Jewish life started and partly because it is the country with the largest Jewish population in the world today. This in turn begs a question about loyalty – my feet may stand in this country, but where does my heart belong? I explain it by describing my priorities when reading the newspaper in the morning: first I look at the front pages and what is happening in this country; then I turn to the back pages and catch up with the sports news. When I then turn to the middle pages and foreign affairs, I am more interested in what is going on in Israel than, say, Uruguay or Japan. I think that holds true for most other British Jews.

Religion and society

There are constant complaints in religious circles about how secular society has become. I am not entirely sure. Take two examples. The first is the fascinating rise of Sunday Assemblies. These are groups of local people who are totally secular, yet who meet in rented halls on Sunday mornings to sing songs (but not hymns), read poetry (but not biblical verses), listen to talks (but not sermons) and share a light meal afterwards (but with no grace before breaking bread). What this new movement shrieks out is that, actually, many of the structures of faith are valuable, even if people no longer follow the theology that accompanies them. What they want is the best of religion – communal rituals, interpersonal camaraderie, a sense of purpose, an ethical framework, challenging moral debates – without the aspects that seem to them either fantastical or obnoxious.

In a similar vein, there are many who reject the answers offered by religion – be it notions of the Trinity or laws over kosher food – but who still ask the same big questions that religion tries to address: Who am I? What is the point of my life? How do I fit into this vast universe? What will happen when I die? Some ask alone, others search through New Age groups, meditation, yoga or various therapies. Both the Sunday Assemblies and the secular seekers could be viewed as a terrible indictment on the failure of organised religion to speak to contemporary needs, or they could be seen as a wonderful opportunity for faith groups to reassess their approach. Normal activities can continue, but space could be made for those who are not believers but who do want a vehicle for meeting and searching, who wish to have the warmth of human contact and a chance to share intelligent discussion. This possibility is all the more timely as churches and other religious buildings are increasingly becoming one of the few accessible public venues, with the demise of local pubs, halls and village shops in rural areas, while larger towns can seem impersonal and lacking any focal point.

The second example is in the extraordinary transformation that is taking place in the dates we observe. At first glance it seems that the religious calendar is slipping away, with few references in printed diaries to the sacred occasions that used to punctuate it, such as Ash Wednesday or Maundy Thursday. Only Easter and Christmas appear to be worth a mention. Instead, a parallel calendar has developed that fills the months, including New Year's Eve, Burns Night, Valentines Day, Mother's Day, St George's Day, April Fool's Day, Father's Day, Halloween, Guy Fawkes, Remembrance Sunday, Thanksgiving, Diwali, and, the latest addition, Black Friday. Some of these had religious origins, but have been secularised with new meanings; others are imports that reflect our increasingly diverse population; yet others are commercial rebrands of earlier traditions. But what is so striking is that in many ways this new calendar replicates exactly the same set of religious feelings that today's society thinks it has outgrown.

Wherever you are at New Year's Eve – pub, party or in bed – it is hard not to think about beginnings and endings, sigh a little over mistakes made and hurts received, as well as look ahead and quietly make resolutions. It is a time of death and rebirth, of loss and renewal (and that sounds fairly religious to me). Once you peer underneath the surface froth of Valentine's Day, what is so engaging is that it celebrates one of the most powerful emotions we possess – the love of one person for another – and so much more positive than its rivals, fear and greed. It resonates as much with teenagers as with octogenarians, and puts on a pedestal the best that love involves: passion, commitment and loyalty (which, dare I point out, are strong religious values too).

Similarly, secular citizens may have abandoned many religious rituals, yet instinctively feel the need to create others when expressing personal relationships: from cards and flowers at Mother's Day, to a bottle of something at Father's Day. It is perilously close to "Thou shalt honour thy father and mother". Halloween may have been overtaken by outlandish costumes, but there is no disguising the deeper theme of good and evil, and the choices we have to make between pursuing a life of righteousness or following powers of darkness. Whether we believe in an external devil or an inclination to make bad choices, we need an annual reminder as to how thin is the line that divides our capacity for giving full throttle to the best in us or the worst in us. Fireworks may dominate Guy Fawkes, but a more considered view of the day reveals themes of political intrigue mixed with religious zealotry that are not limited to the seventeenth century. Once the rockets have fizzed away, it is a salutary reminder of how faith can be a force for both good and bad. The renewed observance of Remembrance Sunday – especially at station concourses or at football matches – after a period in which it lapsed from public consciousness, touches another religious vein: the sacrifice individuals make for a higher cause, and how the greater good can take precedence over self-survival.

Taken together, these and other dates, not only mirror religious sentiments, but imitate the role of the religious calendar in three ways. First, it structures time, turns its endless passage into manageable units, gives them names, and brings time under our control. Second, it gives meaning to those days, investing them with the emotions that affect us, from sadness to celebration, and makes us feel we have a personal stake in them.

Third, the calendar brings us together with others, so that we are not alone and isolated, but form a community of individuals, be it in places of worship or elsewhere: singing "Auld Lang Syne", attending bonfire parties or standing together for a moment's silence. A shared calendar means social camaraderie. Of course, for those of faith, then our own festive list already provides a year-long vehicle for expressing both the intellectual reflections and emotional needs of individuals. It also offers a way of binding families together, as well as creating a sense of wider cohesion. No wonder those without a religious calendar seem to be unconsciously reinventing it. Its value may be much more than even its adherents realise.

It would only be fair to say that the secular world has had an influence on Jewish life. This has most obviously been in the changes in social attitudes to issues such as being gay or trans. Judaism, along with other religions, has been forced to re-evaluate previous (predominantly hostile) attitudes in these areas, albeit with a marked difference between the liberal and orthodox groupings within each faith. The former has accepted that there can be many forms of sexual or gender identity, and all are God-given, whereas the latter has not. (This is explored much more fully in my book *Inclusive Judaism*, co-authored with David Mitchell.) But secular life has also had an impact on the festivals in that nearly every one has been invested with a new meaning. The historic themes still remains intact, but a new aspect has been added alongside it that resonates more with the current climate.

This has not been the result of any rabbinic enclave, nor a systematic review by the laity, but it has happened very spontaneously. One example is *Sukkot*/the Feast of Tabernacles, which also occurs in September. It is officially about the Israelites living in temporary accommodation during the forty years wandering in the wilderness. However important that period may have been, it is the far-off past, with very little connection to the present. Over the last two decades, the festival has been revamped by synagogues throughout the country and turned into an opportunity to think about those who are without a roof over their head today: the homeless and modern wanderers. This in turn has led to food being brought to services, which is then taken to the local food bank, while in many communities it has led them to run weekly lunches for the homeless. The ancient Israelites have not been forgotten, but remembering them has impelled Jews today to also be pro-active on behalf of the contemporary equivalents.

Another instance is *Hanukkah* (the Feast of Dedication) in December. It is still about the Maccabees and their struggle to maintain religious freedom, but the festival has been transformed from an internal Jewish celebration to a showpiece to the wider world. *Hanukkah* candelabra lighting ceremonies now take place at Downing Street with the Prime Minister, as well as a public lighting in Trafalgar Square with the Mayor of London, and similarly in other regional centres. It has become the festival by which we share Jewish values and how we tell the rest of the world about our carefully honed balancing act: standing up for our identity, yet also being part of wider society.

To be honest, *Tu B'Shvat*/the New Year for Trees, crucial back in the fifth century, has lost much of its relevance for a largely non-agricultural community today. However, it has been given a modern update by being turned into Judaism's "green festival". Based on the command in the Bible not to cut down fruit-bearing trees, but to protect the land for the generations to come, it now preaches environmental awareness and our role as stewards, not owners, of the earth. It is all very David Attenborough, but rooted in Jewish tradition.

Meanwhile, *Rosh Hodesh* – which marks the appearance of a new Hebrew month – has been rescued from almost total obscurity. Almost no one kept it, until it was remembered that traditionally women did not work that day. It has since become a woman's festival, with women-only study groups, where they learn together, share experiences and help empower female involvement in synagogue life. These modernisations, inspired by a popular desire for relevance, demonstrate how the festivals can be both preserved and rebranded, so as to keep an ancient faith as fresh as possible.

Chapter 9

Ouch! The Difficult Bits

Conversion... and antisemitism

One of the most fascinating rabbinic tasks is dealing with people who wish to convert to Judaism. It begs the question: why on earth do they want to do it? Yes, there are many great aspects to the faith, but being Jewish automatically means being subject to various degrees of antisemitism. This may be relatively mild today compared to the terrible massacres of the past and instead we just suffer the odd cutting remark or unpleasant joke – but who knows when the previous persecution may return? Personally I reckon that England is one of the most tolerant countries in the world and count myself very lucky to be living here at this time, but Jewish history suggests a pattern of golden ages followed by decline and catastrophes. The causes may differ from country to country – religious hatred, racial prejudice, economic woes, government scapegoating, political machinations, anti-Zionism – but the effect is the same. As someone once put it so elegantly: "the only reason for antisemitism is the existence of the Jews." Breathing was crime enough! It has been described as the longest hatred, or the virus that never disappears, but just goes underground for a while and then returns. As a child growing up, I took it for granted that there was a low-lying level of antisemitism that might not involve riots or expulsions, but would always mean I was regarded as slightly different by contemporaries. This would not impede having non-Jewish friends or being involved in wider society, but I would always be in the eyes of others as, at best, Jewish, and at worst, the Jew.

I am sure this feeling was partly influenced by being the son of a refugee from Nazi Germany. A childhood memory is of seeing a photograph album of my mother's family, all of whom had been killed in the Holocaust. It explained why, unlike many of my school friends, I did not have a host of aunts, uncles and cousins. I also recall being told how important it is to always have one's passport up to date and keep some money in the house that was never used, just in case one had to flee quickly and go elsewhere without any time to prepare or take possessions. However, it was not just an inherited feeling, but learnt from my own experience at an early age. When I was around ten, I was beaten up at school by a gang of others simply because I was Jewish. In my mid teens, at my next school, I also got into a fight, this time initiated by me, because someone made antisemitic comments that I was not prepared to ignore. I have not experienced any physical violence since then, but very occasional comments about "you people" have been periodic reminders that a certain disdain exists even in the most polite quarters.

I am pleased to say that none of my sons has had the same experience, although one of them did have an indirect brush with stereotyping. The primary school which he attended was approached by a film company that was shooting a documentary nearby about the Holocaust. There was a scene in which Jewish children appeared in the background and they approached the school to ask whether they had any Jewish children they could supply, which would help them, while it would be fun for the pupils to see how a film gets made. The school passed the request on to us, his parents, and we gave permission for him to participate. However, the film director decided not to take him after all, because he had blond hair and blue eyes and so, in their eyes, was not Jewish-looking. The son of two rabbis was not Jewish enough! What a shame the director chose to reinforce the stereotype rather than break it.

I know that some of the children at the Synagogue have had difficult encounters. I always do a session each year at the

Religion School for the 12–13 year olds on antisemitism, so that they are prepared for what might lie ahead, can talk about any incidents that may have already occurred, can share any worries and discuss strategies as to how best deal with whatever comes their way. Each year, the reaction is the same: half the class do not have a clue as to what I am talking about and look at me as if I am mad. This is wonderful, exactly how it should be, and I am delighted. The other half have suffered some name-calling or bullying. It tends to be sporadic, rather than ongoing, and the schools, if informed, are usually very good at putting a stop to it.

So why do converts want to put themselves on the frontline? In addition, they take on several prohibitions (giving up pork) and various obligations (days off work for major festivals). There is a huge investment of time, as the conversion course is a minimum of twelve months so as to experience a whole cycle of the year and also have enough time to learn about all the traditions. For, as will be obvious already, being Jewish is not just a matter of believing, but also of doing: whether it be the rituals or the food rules or learning Hebrew or mastering the many dos and don'ts. Anyone who disparages converts, as some people do, is failing to appreciate the enormous commitment that is involved. There are several motives for the desire to change faith, by far the most common being coming into contact firsthand with Jewish family life by having a Jewish partner. In half the cases, the person converts before marriage, having decided that it is important to have a unified family faith. In the other half, they decide after several years of marriage and having lived a Jewish-style life, that they wish to adopt it for themselves. A much smaller number of cases are where someone comes to Judaism without any such ties, but is attracted to its beliefs and values. Curiously enough, there is a divided opinion amongst rabbis to the latter group. Some consider them to be more sincere, as they have no personal relationship that might be influencing them; others reckon it is harder for them to become Jewish as they lack a family to help them integrate. It highlights the fact that, unlike some faiths, being Jewish is not so much an individual journey, but a communal experience. The emphasis is as much on feeling at home within Jewish circles as it is about adhering to a belief system.

The predominance of the "marriage motive" (whether it be before or after the wedding) is why those converting to Judaism tend to be in their twenties and thirties. People do convert at other ages, but not in such great numbers. There is also a much higher number of women who convert than men. This is partly because the tradition of circumcision is something that many men wish to avoid. It is fine when eight days old and you are oblivious to what is going on, but much less appealing when much older and more conscious of sexual performance. As it happens, adult circumcision does not limit the latter in any way, but it is one thing me telling that to a twenty-seven-year old and another thing him deciding to risk it. Exemptions are permitted for those who cannot be circumcised for medical or psychological reasons, but the numbers remain low. Another factor is that for many centuries, Jewish law has stipulated that a child's Jewish status goes through the maternal line. So if a Jewish woman married a non-Jewish man, their children will be Jewish whether he converts or not. If it is the other way round, though, the child will not be Jewish unless the woman converts. For those for whom having Jewish children is important, this is a crucial factor. Both Reform and Liberal Judaism have now altered this law to make it gender neutral: we hold that so long as one parent is Jewish and the children have a Jewish upbringing, then they have Jewish status. Orthodox Judaism still maintains the matrilineal rule.

Another curiosity is that compared to other faiths, Judaism is bottom of the league table when it comes to welcoming, or even wanting, converts. This is partly because the rabbis never claimed we were the only true faith and long ago (i.e. the second century) recognised that other faiths were valid too. To put what they said in colloquial English rather than ancient Hebrew: there are many paths to Heaven and it does not matter which one you take. I know that sounds very modern, but it was written almost two thousand years ago and one of the reasons that I am pleased to be Jewish, for although there are lots of rules and regulations that can sometimes seem pedantic, in the big issues – such as religious tolerance – it has got it right. There was no need, therefore, to be Jewish to reach heaven or be considered a good person in this world. This was reinforced in later periods when Jews were living in Christian or Muslim countries and were banned by law from converting others, with severe penalties being imposed. In addition, the massive social gulf that developed in times of persecution meant that non-Jews rarely considered crossing over, while Jews viewed anyone who did with great suspicion.

The ban on converting others to Judaism may now have been lifted, but the reluctance to proselytise remains. It has become the norm within Orthodoxy, for instance, to automatically turn down someone who wants to convert and only consider their application if they return after three rebuffs. Officially, that is to test their sincerity. Unofficially, it reflects the attitude that unless someone is prepared to keep 100% of the commands – and there are not just the ten famous ones, but 613 in all – then it is better the person stays as they are. "Better a non-Jew than a bad Jew" is the attitude. Reform and Liberal rabbis take a more welcoming approach. That is in keeping with our philosophy that Judaism is not a matter of "all or nothing", but there are many different ways of being Jewish. I would also argue that it is a more honest and certainly more historical position, for Judaism has constantly changed over the centuries and, far from being a monolithic tradition, has adapted to different environments and changing social patterns. Moses would feel a complete stranger if he witnessed first-century Judaism, while the rabbis from that period would feel totally out of place amongst tenth-century colleagues and the latter would feel alien to those in the nineteenth century. The myth of undiluted tradition that orthodoxies of all faiths claim is as daft as those thinking that the St James Bible is the ultimate authority when it is only a sixteenth-century translation of a much earlier original.

Something that has not changed as much as it should is the negativity of some ordinary Jews towards converts. Strangely, it is more amongst those who are lapsed. Religious Jews tend to appreciate the journey they have taken. After all, is it not a massive compliment that someone wants to join your group? For Jews whose attachment is more social and cultural, someone coming from outside can feel different and "not one of us". It is almost an inversion of antisemitism! In addition, those whose own Jewish knowledge is poor and the relic of a half-baked education way back in childhood, can feel threatened by converts who have studied intensely as adults and who end up with a much greater and more sophisticated understanding. One of the unexpected side effects of people with a Jewish partner converting is that, because we also ask the partner to join them on the course, we end up with a tranche of much better educated born Jews. In fact, the result of the year-or-more long tuition often results in both partners becoming involved in synagogue leadership afterwards, whether teaching at the Religion School with their newfound knowledge, serving on one of the committees or being part of the security team.

The existence of that team is a sad reflection on the changed atmosphere in recent decades. After the Second World War, the world recoiled in horror at what Jews had suffered. After the 1970s, though, antagonistic attitudes to the State of Israel spilled over into attacks on Jewish communities, especially in Europe. There has long been a debate as to whether anti-Zionism is the same as antisemitism. In theory, it is possible to be opposed to aspects of the State of Israel, but not be prejudiced against Jews. If anti-Zionism means opposing policies of the particular government in office in Jerusalem, then that is fine, and half of all Israelis are too! But if it means being opposed to the existence of the State of Israel and denying the right to a Jewish homeland, whereas all other people are entitled to their own, then it is clearly a cover for antisemtisim. If opposing Israel entails bombing synagogues in France or Germany, then that too is proof that those anti-Zionists are antisemitic.

Thankfully, despite more minor incidents, such violence has been absent in England, but it would be complacent to think it could not happen here, be it by an organised terrorist group or a lone wolf. Deterrence is a key part of security, and so most synagogues have a team of volunteers standing outside when events take place inside. No one pretends they could prevent a carefully planned armed attack, but even the simple act of locking the front door and calling the police immediately can make a difference between there being major casualties or only a few. It is very sad that we even need to consider such precautions, though – so far – they have not been proved necessary. I also note that most weeks the local paper, the *Maidenhead Advertiser*, reports that a children's playground or bus stop has been subject to mindless vandalism. In addition, the mosque is an occasional target, while churches are sometimes broken into by thieves. Jews can certainly be victims, but we are not the only ones. I was very pleased, for instance, that when the local mosque was subject to bricks being thrown at its window and a security rota was arranged for the following week, a number of those from the synagogue team volunteered to join it.

To complete the story: what happens to converts later on? Does their initial burst of enthusiasm carry on throughout the succeeding years or, like someone who takes up a new hobby, does it tail off after a while? The answer is simple: it varies enormously. Some become stalwarts within the community and a regular presence, whether it be in the services or other aspects. Others express their Jewishness more through home life. Others feel that, having spent such an intense time of study and attendance gaining Jewish status, they can now enjoy being Jewish in a more relaxed way, remaining members but making only occasional appearances. With some justification, they reckon they have earned the right to be like most born Jews! Those who think this is a sign of insincerity are missing the point: if being Jewish was primarily a matter of worship, three-quarters of the community (including some of those critics) would be disqualified. Instead, we are a glorious combination of competing identities – religious, cultural, social, ethnic – that defy neat definition, and being Jewish is best left as a wonderful tapestry of colourful threads that track their own course but also overlap. When someone converts, they jump into that melee, and we should just be grateful that they find it attractive enough to want to be part of it in some way.

There is also the question of whether, if a person converts because of their partner, what happens when there is a divorce or death? There are no set patterns, but if the former is a particularly acrimonious split, the person who converted is more likely to leave Judaism as it is one of many ways of rejecting everything associated with their ex. Cutting ties with his/her family, chucking their clothes out of the window, puncturing their car wheels and rejecting their god are all options to which some divorcees resort. A death can have a very different effect, and there have been numerous cases where the Jewish partner in a mixed-faith marriage dies and the non-Jewish spouse decides to convert as a way of maintaining the link with him/her. They had never pursued conversion during the thirty or forty years of marriage, but now feel the need to do so. In fact, one of the cases I turned down was that of a non-Jewish 26-year-old whose Jewish fiancé had been killed in a car crash two months earlier and wanted to convert. She said she wanted to be as close as possible to him and his lifestyle. I had no doubt she meant it, but it was not the right course for her. Effectively, she was not letting go of him and trying to keep the relationship with him alive. I though it best she stayed as she was, grieved, slowly moved on and (although I did not say this to her) met someone else. If he turned out to be Jewish too, she could always convert then. She was very upset at my refusal, but I am sure it was the right decision.

Of course, conversion can be a two-way process, and there have been a couple of members who have left Judaism and adopted another faith. Part of me felt sad that we were not providing what they needed, but part of me was pleased that at least they had found a religious home elsewhere. As intimated above, Judaism does not have a problem with other faiths, with the only criterion for acceptance being that they have a moral basis. In both my cases, they adopted Christianity, having encountered it through the influence of friends and found it attractive. I do not consider the slightly larger number of members who describe themselves as Buddhist to have converted away from Judaism, as they see themselves as attached to both. This is part of a much wider phenomenon in British Jewry at large, and even more so in the USA, where their ability to combine both traditions has earned them the title of being a JuBu. They tend to regard Buddhism as a "spiritual top-up" to their Jewish roots and have no problem still paying an annual subscription to the Synagogue.

Media matters

Another activity outside the synagogue building, but which I would still count as congregational duties is working with the media, be it newspapers, radio, television or, more recently social media. It is a way of spreading knowledge about Judaism to those who have little knowledge, or misconceptions, about it. It is also a means of reaching Jews in the area who either are not aware there is a synagogue locally or who do know, but do not think it has anything positive to offer them. It was also something I enjoyed, be it writing articles or doing broadcasts. I quickly realised, though, that very different skills are needed from congregational life. When dealing with members, I always tried to see their point of view, suggest compromises in order to move forwards and act as a bridge between opposing opinions. In contrast, media debates often demand hard-edged positions, argued definitively, picking holes in opponents and not giving ground. Some programmes do permit reasoned discussion and seeking nuances, such as Radio 4's *Beyond Belief*. Others, such as BBC television's *Kilroy* or *The Big Questions* are a bear-pit in which you have to fight to get your voice heard and then argue your case forcefully.

I realised how one can easily overstep the mark following an episode of the latter in which I challenged a young priest who had claimed that at Catholic schools subjects such as abortion and homosexuality were discussed in a free and open way. I started my riposte by saying, "If I believed you for one second, and I would not give you any more time than that." When the debate then went on to discuss the merits or otherwise of faith schools, I told him: "Your saviour, Jesus, said: suffer the little children, not segregate them." A few days later, I received a letter from County Down in Northern Ireland, part of which read: "That was a very good programme and you spoke well. I did not agree with you, but you expressed yourself eloquently, though I wish you had not trashed my son the priest." Fortunately, his address and phone number were on his letterhead, so I rang to apologise for any hurt caused. Needless to say, there were other occasions where I was combatted very powerfully. Such debates are certainly not for the meek and mild.

More enjoyable was the occasion when I was able to combine two loves – the Bible and football. It was at the time of the 1986 World Cup in Mexico and the media had exhausted itself looking at every aspect of the game. There were still a few days to go before the first match, so that left the problem of how to fill the pages? So they turned to religion. I turned down the requests to pray for victory – I do not believe in praying for results, as that is a form of divine match fixing and takes away freewill from those playing on the pitch. Instead, I said that what is acceptable is praying for qualities: that the English players are neither overconfident nor overawed, and can give of their best; that fans can have the self-discipline to be supportive of their team, without being abusive of the other ones; and for them to control their emotions sufficiently so that they can accept defeat without letting their disappointment turn into anger that can lead to violence, be it at the football ground or when they get back home (with domestic retributions on partners or children sometimes occurring). I reckon football can offer a striking image to those of faith, as the two have a curious feature in common. Whatever happens to a team in a season – soaring success or abject failure – it is only temporary and everything starts all over again the following season. So too with us, and the festival of *Yom Kippur* reminds us that we have a chance to re-set our lives and an opportunity to make the coming year a better year.

In a more light-hearted vein, I also referred the journalists to the Bible for some advice. For instance, if a free kick is given against them near their goal, they should pay attention to Nahum 2.5: "They shall make haste to the wall and the defence shall be prepared", and also trust that Proverbs 1.17 applies to their opponents: "Surely in vain the net is spread in sight". There is advice, too, for the English coach if an injury occurs, namely: "to loose his shoe from off his foot" (Deuteronomy 25.9), while the referee is urged to deal firmly with any delaying tactics: "He shall pay for the loss of time" (Exodus 21.19). I also hoped that the English captain, Bryan Robson, never has cause to use Psalm 139.16 to the referee: "In thy book, all my members are written", nor that any English player has to admit that Psalm 38.16 had come to pass – "when my foot slips, they magnify themselves against me". I concluded by urging English fans to join the manger, Bobby Robson, in chanting Psalm 116.13: "I will lift up the cup". While I was keen to watch what happened on the pitch, my own personal goal was to study the fans, and try to work out how to transfer the passionate support and exuberant singing of those attending football matches to those who come to services. The result? Work in progress!

Like the fish that got away, the best programmes were those that never reached the screen. After he wrote his book on *The God Delusion*, I was due to be filmed by the BBC with Richard Dawkins whilst in a hot air balloon floating over Oxford. Presumably, the producer thought it would be a good visual comment, though I was not sure if he was thinking of hot air or heavenly journeys. Unfortunately, ten minutes before filming started, a high wind arose, making the venture impossible. The debate did take place on the ground, but it was deemed to be too ordinary and did not make the final cut. I also missed out on a trip to Iceland, where Channel 4 wanted to do a sequence with Ann Widdecombe and me discussing climate change mid-air whilst flying over glaciers. That, too, fell foul of logistics. The only time, I turned down a programme was when I was invited to be on a special Christmas edition of BBC's *The Weakest Link* with Anne Robinson, to be comprised of clergy from different faiths as the contestants. It was a highly successful but humiliating quiz show in which the worst performing participants are ejected with the merciless admonishment: "You are the Weakest Link". I decided that while I was prepared to publicly argue a cause and go down fighting, this was a form of ritual extinction in front of a few million witnesses that would not serve any ends. I shall leave it to you to decide whether it was cowardice or good sense.

What is noticeable about religion in the media is how often it is portrayed via comedy. Whether it be Derek Nimmo in *All Gas and Gaiters*, Dawn French's *The Vicar of Dibley*, Dermot Morgan as *Father Ted* or Tom Hollander's *Rev*. Humour is certainly a powerful tool that many a preacher employs, but in order to illustrate a serious point, not to be the object of laughs. To be fair, though, in its more serious output, the BBC in particular has done much to introduce representatives from non-Christian faiths to the wider public. It has also destroyed many stereotypes. Those who may have associated Sikhs primarily with militant violence in the Punjab, have been forced to re-evaluate their views after being exposed to the gentle wisdom of Indarjit Singh. Those who imagined rabbis as bearded foreigners divorced from everyday life have had to cope with clean-shaven Oxford graduate Lionel Blue and his homely anecdotes. The BBC has also been an agent for change. I have met more imams and bishops in television studios than ever I would have done in the high street. It has created an interfaith media community that has led to a cross-fertilisation of ideas and personalities that might otherwise never have happened.

Writing articles started when I was nine or ten years old and wrote regularly for a children's magazine about animals and have been scribbling ever since. Over the years, I have written for many papers, from *The Times* to the *Daily Mail*, and magazines from *The Spectator* to *Cosmopolitan*. There was one title that had eluded me, *The Big Issue*, and then the commission came. For a week my words of wisdom were being touted (with those of others) on every street corner, and the following week they made good wrapping paper for fish and chips. Seeing your by-line sticking out of a rubbish bin smeared in tomato ketchup is a great antidote for the ego. As for books, I may be letting myself in for some searing rebukes, but I always think that producing a book – conceiving the idea, carrying it around with us in our heads over several months, then eventually getting it out of us into print and letting it loose on the world – is the nearest thing we blokes come to feeling what it is like to go through having a child. Please note, I did not say it was the same, just the nearest thing we can manage.

My cancer

A few years ago I had a lucky break. I am always telling others to get check-ups, and so I decided that I should follow my own advice and have a prostate cancer test. I had no symptoms whatsoever and saw it as a purely routine blood test to take and then forget about. I was surprised to find that I not only had it, but it was an aggressive cancer and at an advanced level. Within two weeks, I was in hospital having the tumour removed, which was then followed by a six-week course in radiotherapy as a "mopping-up" exercise, as some of the cancer cells had already gone elsewhere. With hindsight, I was pleased by my instant reaction when the consultant first told me the news. I had shrugged my shoulders and said "Well, other people get cancer, so why shouldn't I?" I was pleased because I did not protest, say how unfair it was or question why God had let me down despite all I have done for God. It tied in exactly with my long-held view (but from which I might have departed emotionally in the heat of the moment) that life is not about justice or fairness. Instead, it is full of dangers and random events, as well as wonderful aspects and great acts of love.

If bad things happen, they happen. Sometimes they are the fault of others (a drunken driver), sometimes they are forces of nature (an earthquake), but in neither case are they part of God's will. I do not believe that God micromanages the world, but that we are in charge. Other people can affect us for good or bad, while nature can impact on us with its astonishing beauty or destructive power. Religion is there not to justify the unpleasant or explain the inconsistent, but to help us respond well: by picking ourselves up when knocked down or assisting others who are in distress. It gives us guidance as to how to turn the jungle of this world into a garden and to tame self-centred instincts. For me, religion is about being hands-on, helping us combat whatever we have to face and encouraging us to act in harmony with each other. Cancer is one of those random events that nobody deserves, while it does not indicate divine punishment. So the two questions when we get afflicted with some disease should be: firstly, "Why not me?" and secondly, "What inner strength can I call on to help me deal with it?"

I have witnessed a variety of strategies that members of my community have adopted. For some, the cancer is all-consuming: it dominates their life and their conversation – which is hardly surprising, and maybe it needs every ounce of their energy to combat. However, it does mean that even if the cancer is beaten, it took two or three years of their life that can never be returned. For others, the cancer is seen as a nuisance, an irritant, like a leg wound that makes them limp, but rather than rest their leg all day, they are just as busy as before, albeit limping. They keep doctors' appointments to the edge of their day, carry on working, or pursuing their family commitments, and try to preserve as much of their personal agenda as possible. Others simply collapse and react hysterically, deciding that a tumour is a death sentence. They spend all their time worrying and complaining, like one person who had been told the cancer was terminal, but that she would have at least two years beforehand. Rather than use those two years to see family, mix with friends, travel while still fit and enjoy a hobby – instead she just repeated week after week, "I am going to die, I only have two years left." She totally wasted those two years, and it was as if she never even had them. Others have wild fluctuations, sometimes feeling on top of things and that they are coping well; at other times feeling totally down and that it is not worth carrying on. Ultimately everyone faces the choice of whether they are going to be a cancer sufferer (who has to contend with the disease), or a cancer victim (who is going to fall prey to it even if they recover).

As for what happens next – if there is an afterlife and what does it look like – that is one of the questions that I am often asked, whether or not a person is suffering a life-threatening illness. Once upon a time, everyone believed they had a choice between heaven and hell, now most people are not sure and find the uncertainty very disconcerting. Like television dramas that end episodes by tantalising us with what will take place in next week's programme, we are even more keen to know our own fate. Is there more to come in another world? Or is this it and, like a matchstick that burns out, we lie still forever? Judaism does suggest that there is an afterlife, but does not spell out what it involves. The latter is because we simply do not know, which is true enough, but then logically that should apply to the former too. I know that many of my congregation would like to believe that we continue in some form, and maybe even meet up with loved ones who have passed away. I would like to believe that too, but see no evidence for it. But rather than be depressed by that thought, it inspires me to make the most of the life that I do have, and I urge others to do similarly. The next world may turn out be a glorious reality or a fraudulent religious sales pitch, but in the meantime we should live our potential to the full, albeit in harmony with others so that we do not limit their life chances. So when I am asked about what we can expect after death, I always tell them to concentrate on this world, and leave the next to God. Personally, I will be interested to find out one day myself, but I am not banking on anything. The good news is that if there is nothing, then as we will not know, we will not be disappointed.

It seems, though, that I have lasted longer than some people thought: until the late Lord Sacks was raised to the peerage and got an extra title in front of his name, I was often confused with him, as we were both "Rabbi Dr Jonathan" and both appeared on BBC radio periodically. Every now and then I was congratulated on a broadcast he had made. This was mildly amusing, but reached a different level when he died. At a local interfaith gathering, at which I was not present but my wife attended, the Jewish community was offered sincere condolences on the loss of Rabbi Dr Jonathan Romain. She was pleased to be able to correct the sad news. I can now echo Mark Twain's "the reports of my death are greatly exaggerated" (so far).

Chapter 10

Fifteen Minutes of Fame (x 4)

Mixed-faith couples

If Andy Warhol was right that one day we would each have fifteen minutes of fame, then I have been fortunate to have four mini-doses on the national stage. Each was highly controversial at the time, although events subsequently vindicated all four stands. The first was with regard to mixed-faith couples, though I should warn you that what may seem obvious now was revolutionary back in the 1980s. I had run a series of evenings for my own members at Maidenhead on different themes that I thought would be of interest to individuals in those situations, such as bereavement, divorce and problem teenagers. They all received a decent turnout, but the one on mixed-faith marriage was crowded out, while I had people calling up from all over South East England who had somehow heard about it. I realised I had uncovered an issue that needed far greater attention. At that time, as mentioned in the first chapter, mixed-faith relationships were rocketing. They were the subject of much angst within Jewish families and were fiercely condemned by both the rabbinic establishment and communal leaders. Moreover, this was not just a Jewish concern, but similar ructions were occurring in other faith groups. Social barriers were crumbling, while members of different religions were meeting at university, work or leisure activities. For the individuals involved it was simply a matter of falling in love, but it was seen by others as rejection of their faith and upbringing. The result was a great deal of personal unhappiness, while rabbis and other clergy were increasingly fearful of losing their flock.

I decided to hold national seminars open to all mixed-faith couples, initially in London, but also in major cities such as Manchester, Glasgow and Bristol. They were based on the view that, whether others liked it or not, such unions existed and would increase. The object was not to split them up, but help them tackle the issues they faced, be it dealing with upset relatives, arranging an inclusive wedding day, establishing a home that respected both religious cultures (e.g., domestic ceremonies or food laws) and agreeing how best to raise the children. There were no assumptions as to the "right way", but an attempt to get the couples themselves to work out what would work best for them and their particular situation. It was up to them, for instance, if they were to have a baby boy whether to circumcise him, baptise him, do neither or both. The key point was to discuss this and all other issues in advance, so that there were no unexpected hiccups or running arguments. The seminars also had a separate track for the parents of mixed-faith couples, in order to give them a chance to express their feelings and then discuss how best to come to terms with the reality they faced. They had less options and, ultimately either had to accept the couple or shun their offspring's decision, but what was important was for them to realise that loving someone from another faith did not mean loving their parents any less. At the same time, the seminars gave a message to the religious authorities: previous social patterns were changing and although they might still wish to encourage people to marry within their faith, fulminating against those who chose not to do so did not affect the trend and only succeeded in alienating an increasingly large number of members. It would be far better to say, for instance, "Okay, this is not our first choice, but you are still Jewish (or Catholic or Muslim or whatever) and still welcome, while your partner will be treated with every respect."

The seminars were wildly successful, attracted hundreds of participants and I ran them for the next twenty-five years. It was not just engaged couples who came, but also those long married who had never had the chance to talk about their situation before in a sympathetic environment. Many were overwhelmed when they came through the doors and suddenly realised they were not alone, which they had often been made to feel. It was very noticeable that the issues and dilemmas faced by the Jewish partners were exactly the same as those faced by the other partner in his/her own family and faith community. How do we marry not only two individuals, but two different ways of running a home and bringing up children? How to accommodate two faiths without negating either or both? In this respect, it was critical to appreciate that even if the couple did not consider themselves particularly observant, they were still the product of religious cultures. Moreover, while this might not seem very pronounced to them whilst young and single, its impact would become much stronger once they had a home of their own and children.

One of the most powerful features to arise was that the issue couples agonised most over was the effect of their marriage on any children. The way forward that helped them most was my suggestion to distinguish between religious status (what the children were officially in the eyes of a particular faith), religious identity (how the children saw themselves) and religious education (the knowledge they had of one or both faiths). There were several different computations possible in handling each aspect, according to what was most appropriate for the couple. For instance, a child could have the status of one faith, the identity of the other, and education in both. What worked best was whatever the format the couple had discussed and agreed upon. Two other strong themes emerged: one was that virtually all couples said they had never intended marrying someone of a different faith, but it just happened that way. The other was that many of the Jewish partners reckoned they felt more Jewish as a result of marrying a non-Jew, as it forced them to keep alive traditions they might not have bothered with, but now knew depended on them to maintain. One other curiosity that emerged was the disproportionately high percentage of Jews whose partners were Catholic, far higher than what would be expected given the paucity of both groups. Some joked that it was because they both shared a strong sense of guilt inculcated in them. Personally, I suspect it may be more to do with both having in common a strong sense of family and home life underneath the surface differences, while the fact that both are minorities means there is a shared perspective on the rest of society: in it but not entirely of it.

The seminars attracted national attention, being the first to highlight the theme of mixed-faith relationships in Britain. The result was many radio debates, television appearances and newspaper articles. Eventually it led to an MBE for trying to tackle the subject positively and help those concerned. However, it also aroused great controversy, especially amongst the ecclesiastical establishment of several faiths. Within the Jewish community, I was accused of "doing Hitler's work for him" by hastening the extinction of the Jewish race. I was condemned by others for "giving the green light to assimilation". Frankly, I never realised I had such power! I did point out that couples were not suddenly going to marry because a rabbi in Berkshire said he would not shout at them. In the end, even Orthodox rabbis began to realise that I was not encouraging mixed-faith marriage, but responding to it. Local synagogues began to put on their own version of the seminars or to specify that mixed-faith couples were welcome. I brought the national ones to a close as the culture within both British Jewry and wider society had changed completely.

Over the years, four main lessons had arisen: first, that marrying out of the faith did not mean rejecting it, and many were still keen to pursue their religious heritage if they were allowed to do so. Second, mixed-faith marriages did not have a substantially higher rate of divorce; if they failed it was usually to do with the usual problems of false expectations, difficult finances or infidelity. Third, those from Orthodox backgrounds were no less likely to "marry out" than those from Reform ones; it was a national scenario from which no group was immune, save those who totally isolated themselves from the rest of society. Fourth, it is not the fault of parents for neglecting their child's religious education; it happens as much where families have sent their children to Sunday classes, faith schools, youth clubs or summer camps; these may strengthen their religious identity but do not stop them mixing with others when they emerge into the wider world and form relationships.

Faith Schools

My second brush with the headlines was over faith schools. I was disturbed by their increasing growth within the Jewish community. Whereas one in five children attended Jewish schools in the 1970s, by 2008 the proportion was almost two-thirds. Previously, the pupils had primarily come from very Orthodox households, now they were the norm for Jewish children from all types of backgrounds. It meant that the community at large was becoming increasingly divorced from wider society: the children were not mixing with each other, while parents were not meeting outside the school gate, at PTAs, the school play or sports days. It was not a healthy development, because lack of contact would inevitably mean lack of knowledge of each other's ways, or what they had in common. Ignorance could then spiral into suspicion and then deteriorate into hostility. This was not the intention behind the growth of Jewish schools, but it was the consequence. Instead, the motive was partly because it was felt that Jewish children were not receiving sufficient religious education from the home or Sunday classes and so they needed to be "re-Judaized". It was also an attempt to combat the rising level of mixed-faith marriage by instilling a greater sense of Jewish commitment.

At the same time, the Blair Government (1997 to 2007) was

encouraging the growth of faith schools among all religious
groups through its Academy schools initiative. There had
always been a high number of Christian-based schools, mainly
Church of England, but also a significant number of Catholic
ones, and now there was a small but steady rise in Muslim
schools, while the first Hindu and Sikh ones started. It meant
that families throughout the country were being increasingly
divided into faith groups, not just in their personal practices, but
through state institutions, and not just at weekends but Monday
to Friday too. What was even more astonishing was that this
was happening at the very same time as a new development in
the opposite direction in Northern Ireland. No one would claim
that separate Protestant and Catholic schools were the cause
of the sectarian violence there, but they certainly perpetuated
the gulf between the two communities. As the peace process
gathered momentum politically, parents realised they had to
break the social fragmentation to underpin it and create a more
tolerant generation. An increasing number were sending their
children to Integrated Schools, where children from both faiths
could mix and grow up together. Yet here we were in the rest
of Britain *creating* religious segregation. What message was it
sending children divided at the school gate other than a "them
and us" culture. The faith schools all claimed they were teaching
tolerance of those who were different, but the reality was they
were isolating children from each other and fine words could
not overcome the physical separation.

I was appalled and spoke in the media about the problems
that we were building up for a new generation that would
emerge estranged from each other. Others felt the same but
there was no vehicle to express our misgivings or to alter
public policy. The result was that I was asked to be Chair of a
campaigning organisation being formed in 2008 by both secular
and religious groups, the Accord Coalition, whose purpose was
to promote inclusive education. It attempted to move beyond

the, till then, simplistic battle lines of those for or against faith schools. Instead, it wanted to find a more nuanced position, which recognised that faith schools were likely to remain an integral part of the educational system (they accounted for a third of all schools), but could be changed in ways that would improve social cohesion.

We initially focused on four main areas. The first was having an open admissions policy that was not determined by a child's faith, but if he/she was local to the school. It meant that state-funded faith schools would be serving the local community, not their own interests. It was tax-payers' money that was funding them, so they had a responsibility to those living locally. Second was not to discriminate in employment policy. It might be reasonable for the RE teacher to be of the faith to which the school adhered, but there was no reason why the Maths teacher, French instructor or Sports coach should be. Insisting on, for instance, all-Jewish or all-Catholic staff not only limited job applications, but also restricted the role models and life views that the pupils encountered. Third, was to ensure that the RE syllabus was objective and broad-based. That meant including coverage of other faiths and non-religious beliefs, as well as different perspectives on ethical issues such as abortion and contraception. At the time of the National Curriculum, RE was the only statutory subject without a place in it, leading to each school operating its own system and able to indoctrinate rather than educate. Fourth was improving accountability, as RE lessons in faith schools were exempt from OFSTED regulations. Instead, RE was overseen by the same faith group that delivered it, so there was no external monitoring. This was an invitation for bad practices (such as misleading information or one-sided guidance) to flourish without being checked and remedied.

I hope the above seem reasonable goals. They were based on the assumption that religious direction is perfectly legitimate when it came from the home or place of worship, but that was not the purpose of schools, especially state-funded ones. Schools should be places which broaden children's minds and challenge their preconceptions. They should also build bridges between the different elements in society, not erect barriers. Precisely because Britain was now a multifaith and multiracial country, it was important to ensure it did not become a multifractured one. The response to Accord, however, was a torrent of condemnation. In a co-ordinated response, the Anglican, Catholic and Jewish faith school providers lambasted us as abhorrent and accused us of denying children the right to a religious education. As outlined in the second sentence of this paragraph, this was patently not true. As the founding chair and main spokesman of Accord, I was personally crucified (well, it felt like that) by the main Jewish newspaper, the *Jewish Chronicle*, which devoted the front page and several more inside to revile me for undermining Jewish life. As it happens, I was chair of the Assembly of Reform Rabbis UK at the time, and my position was called into question, though I did survive attempts to unseat me.

Over the next ten years chair, the period for which I was chair of Accord, it was successful in making the way faith schools were run the subject of national attention. As well as media debates, we spoke at the annual conferences of all three main parties, Conservatives, Labour and Liberal Democrats, as well as the European Parliament and the Church of England Synod. We were also invited to 10 Downing Street to discuss potential policy changes. It is fair to say that although we antagonised many vested interests, we also provided a voice for many ordinary people who were worried by the divisive effect of faith schools. Among our successes were influencing a major change in the curriculum, whereby those taking GCSE RE no longer studied one faith (almost always the faith of their particular school), but had to cover two. We also harnessed a climate of public opinion demanding greater inclusivity in admission procedures and this led to faith-based Free Schools being limited to accepting 50% of their pupils from any one faith. Our *cri de coeur* was that if we want an inclusive and tolerant society, then we have to have an inclusive and tolerant educational system that produces it.

As time progressed, so did our campaigning targets. In the latter years, we argued that the 50% cap should be extended to all faith schools, not just Free ones, so that even if they have a faith ethos, they have a more equal admissions system. We also called for an end to unregistered schools, which applied to all faiths, but particularly to the Jewish and Muslim community. They not only severely limited the education that was provided, but were unhygienic, used corporal punishment and breached many health and safety regulations. It was a public disgrace that their existence had been well known for years by local authorities, but they had turned a blind eye to them.

Assisted Dying

My third national campaign was the matter of life and death, literally. Like most clergy, I regularly visit those who are afflicted with serious illnesses that have no cure and inevitably result in death, such as Motor Neurone Disease or Huntington's. In fact, they have a particularly unpleasant form of death, not only at the very end, but also in the period prior, with severe loss of bodily functions and physical abilities. It is always desperately sad to see once vibrant individuals deteriorate and become incapacitated, and to witness how much they are suffering both physically and mentally. The medical advances that have been made in certain areas have been astonishing – which is why I did not mention cancer just now, as so many people can survive it. Equally amazing is the palliative care on offer, whether through hospices for respite stays or end of life care, or through visiting services such as the Macmillan Nurses, all of which have helped ease that suffering enormously. Yet there is still much pain that cannot be controlled and distress that cannot be assuaged.

I had long been aware of the campaign to allow an assisted death, but had rejected it for all the usual reasons: that it was not up to us to take life, even our own; or that a change in the law, however kindly meant, would be a slippery slope that led to dangerous developments. They were solid arguments and I went along with them. The turning point for me was when I came to see a congregant and found him kneeling on top of his bed, head tucked down, both hands wrapped around his knees and clutching them tightly, all in an effort to control his pain. He died three weeks later in dreadful circumstances. I never said it to his widow, but I did ask myself many times: what was the point of those last three weeks? He was dying, nothing could be done to save him, nor anything to alleviate the pain except giving him so much morphine that he was stupefied out of all cognitive existence. Would it not have been kinder, if it had been legal and if he had so wished, to let him have an assisted death. It would not have been about curtailing his life, but about shortening his death throes. It also occurred to me that it would be a much more religious response: there is nothing sacred about suffering, nothing holy about agony.

But how to reconcile that view with my previous objections? The more I thought about them, the more they evaporated away. Yes, in principle, it is not desirable to end life before its time. But when is that and who decides? Judaism in particular has long opposed taking someone else's life via the death penalty – not in 1965 when it was abolished by Parliament, but back in the second century. What about taking one's own life? Suicide has also been strongly frowned upon, and until recently, as a sign of that disapproval, those who committed suicide were buried in a separate part of Jewish cemeteries and without any mourning rituals. But assisted death was neither of these and it was clear that linguistic laziness – such as describing it as mercy killing, euthanasia or suicide – was confusing the issue. Clarity was vital. Euthanasia was when one person (acting individually or on behalf of the state) killed another person, with or without their consent. Suicide was when one killed oneself – be it out of depression, as a political statement or because of another cause – but would have lived for many more years had one not done so. In complete contrast, assisted dying is when a person who is approaching death takes their own life. The "assisted" part is because they are given a lethal potion, prescribed by a doctor, which they can take by themselves in their own time and with their own free will. I could still oppose euthanasia, and work hard to prevent suicides, but be in favour of assisted dying.

The "slippery slope" argument also melted away in the light of the protections that were being proposed. Assisted dying would not be a free-for-all, but tightly regulated and monitored. If there was to be a change in the law, it would only be for those who had been told by a medical authority that they were dying (defined as within the next six months). They would then have to be interviewed by two independent doctors to check that they were mentally competent, making the decision in the knowledge of palliative care options and doing so without any external pressure. The procedure would also have to be approved by a judge to ensure legal oversight. Once medication had been prescribed, there was no time limit within which to take it, while the person could decide at any point not to proceed. This seemed as watertight a system as there could possibly be, and would have sufficient checks and balances to ensure that nobody was persuaded to opt for an assisted death against their will or obtained it in inappropriate circumstances.

This would protect the mythological little old lady whose evil children were keen to bump her off to obtain her supposed loot. It would also rule out a person who was undergoing a severe depression, but who was physically healthy and might well recover. I must admit that part of me feels that there might be the occasional case when someone should be allowed to apply who is not terminally ill, such as a person who is totally and irrevocably incapacitated in an accident, and does not wish to live on for the next thirty or more years in such a state. But while I feel enormously sympathetic to such terrible situations, it would introduce exceptions that would either be impossible to define legally or would leave the door open to an ever increasing list of "special cases". Far better, therefore, to have a clear benchmark of assisted dying being solely for those already approaching death within a short time.

The result was that I contacted the organisation Dignity in Dying to find out more about their campaign. I was subsequently invited to be on their Board and then became Vice-Chair, under the leadership of Baroness Molly Meacher. It was very apparent that one of the main groups blocking any attempts to allow assisted dying were religious bodies. The hierarchies in particular were solidly opposed, and the combined strength of the Archbishop of Canterbury, Cardinal Archbishop of Westminster and the Chief Rabbi exerted a powerful influence on MPs and the Government. It was equally clear, though, that while they were entitled to their views, they did not represent all people of faith. I therefore founded IFDiD (Inter Faith leaders for Dignity in Dying) – a clergy group of those in favour of assisted dying. Initially it was made up of rabbis and vicars (as well as one bishop), and eventually we were able to expand to include an imam. The object was partly to bring together like-minded individuals who had previously felt marginalised (or even obliged to keep quiet) by the stance of their authorities. It was to be a "safe place" where we could express our opinions and explore ideas. It was also a way of signalling both to our respective flocks and to society at large that there was not a monolithic opposition to assisted dying and that, on the contrary, there were religious voices in favour. We wanted to break the mould, and that certainly happened with great media attention to our formation, along with the expected condemnation by the hierarchies. They realised it was a challenge to the consensus they were pretending existed, and they were not pleased. A major breakthrough moment came in 2014 when the former Archbishop of Canterbury switched sides and dramatically came out in favour of assisted dying. Further evidence of the religious case for a change in the law came with the endorsement of former Archbishop of Cape Town, Desmond Tutu.

Unfortunately, the intervention of such major figures did not shift the religious hierarchies, but they did highlight the diversity of views amongst people of faith and showed that the religious lobby was not as strong as it thought it was. This was given a significant boost by polling results. It had long been known that the population at large was in favour of the law being changed. A poll conducted by Populus in April 2019 not only showed overwhelming support among the public, with the astonishing figure of 84% in favour, but it was also the case among the majority of those who were religious (defined by attending a place of worship at least once a month). It did vary according to the faiths, with the breakdown being:

Christian 82%
Muslim 37%
Hindu 83%
Jewish 71%
Sikh 84%
Buddhist 84%

The huge disparity between the views of the religious leadership and those of the religious membership begged the question of why there was still such opposition from on high, to which there has been no satisfactory answer, save the power of conformity to tradition.

It is not only bishops who are reluctant to change, so too

are MPs, and although bills in favour have been passed in the House of Lords, they have all failed so far in the Commons. Clearly there are those who are opposed to it as a matter of principle, but there are two other groups who have voted it down. One is those who have not had time to scrutinise the legislation properly and are simply not aware of the protections that have been built into the proposals and are nervous of change. The other is those who are fearful of being labelled by opponents as "permissive" or the "death MP". There is no doubt that changing the law would be a major departure from the past, but I am sure that it would be a beneficial change. I am equally convinced that, once enacted, most people will reckon: "why on earth did it take so long? – we should have done it long ago." This is not a case of me being over-confident, but the result of something that I would not normally dare to say in print or aloud: that in respect to assisted dying we can see the future. This is because while a change in the law would be new for the UK, almost exactly the same form of legislation was passed in the State of Oregon in 1997. It means that, at the time of writing, we have nearly twenty-five years' worth of data to mull over and analyse.

Two major trends have emerged. First, that although thousands of people apply for the right to an assisted death, very few take it up, around 0.4% of the total number of deaths. In 2017 this meant 143 people out of 36,498 who died in Oregon. Moreover, this has been a consistently low figure over the last two decades. Thus the fact that it is available does not mean it is used, and it serves an important role as a psychological safety net, with people having the comfort of knowing they can take the option if life becomes unbearable, but usually do not pursue it. The second trend is that those who do take it up are often well educated and affluent people, who have been used to controlling all aspects of their life, and who wish to control their death as well, especially if they view a debilitating and painful end as a travesty of all that has happened up till then. What has transpired in Oregon – facts on the ground as opposed to speculation – is the best answer to those who are worried, or who deliberately peddle worries, about the consequences of introducing assisted dying over here. There is every reason, therefore, to expect that there would be great interest in it, but little take-up, save for those for whom it means the difference between dying in pain or dying well. For me, that is sufficient grounds for permitting it, from both a practical and a religious perspective.

Jeremy Corbyn

My fourth engagement with controversy was over an individual, rather than a cause. I had not been desperately impressed by Jeremy Corbyn when he was elected leader of the Labour Party in 2015, but did not think too much more about the matter. It was a party decision, and although I watched political events closely, I had never been directly involved in them. The only aspect that worried me slightly was the almost cult-like following he seemed to have, with chants of "Oooh – Jeremy Corbyn" permeating his rallies. It seemed an unhealthy departure from the previous way of doing politics in Britain. Being versed in the Bible meant that I had a keen sense of idolatry, and the euphoric reaction to Corbyn smacked of political idolatry, which could be even more dangerous than its religious cousin. His sudden change from obscure backbencher to potential Prime Minister meant that much of his past began to surface, and the more that was revealed, the more disquieting the picture became. This applied to his support for the IRA's campaign of violence during the Troubles, or his idealisation of the Venezuelan political system despite its economic and moral bankruptcy. It was also apparent in his attitude to Israel. He claimed to be passionate about bringing peace to the area, but consistently vilified Israel and refused to meet with Israelis, but fully supported Palestinian groups and met with members of terrorist organisations. Working for peace means working with both sides.

It should be stated very clearly that there is nothing wrong with taking sides in the Middle East conflict, nor in blaming Israel for the mistakes it has made over the years. In fact, the greatest critics of Israel are Israelis themselves, with every election in recent decades showing the country is deeply divided between left and right, between those committed to pursuing the peace process and those who have given up on it, between those keen to expand Israeli settlements in the West bank and those wanting to withdraw them. The problem with Corbyn's stance was that it was totally one-sided, unwilling to engage even with Israelis on the left or Israeli peace groups, and refusing to condemn the Palestinians for atrocities they had unleashed. His uncritical support for Hamas and Hezbollah was puzzling on another level too, given that they limited women's equality, did not tolerate gay rights, and spurned a democratic system of governance. By contrast, Israel championed all three causes.

Up to this point, Corbyn may have held views that many British Jews deemed unpalatable, but he was entitled to his opinion and that was that. However, two further developments began to ring alarm bells. The first was that it seemed increasingly clear that he did not just object to Israeli policies, but to Israel's existence itself. Yes, let the Palestinians have greater rights within Israel, or their own homeland entirely, but why should Israel suddenly evaporate? What is more, Corbyn was a great champion of the United Nations and letting it decide matters of conflict. Yet he ignored the fact that whereas many countries have come into being through war and conquest, Israel was voted into existence by the United Nations and through international agreement. In that sense, it has more legitimacy than most other countries, especially those in the Middle East, which were often the result of colonial carve-ups. It would be perfectly reasonable for Corbyn to oppose Israeli policies and to excoriate particular Israeli governments, but to deny Israel's right to exist was astonishing.

The second development was the growing suspicion that Corbyn was not only anti-Israel, but anti-Jewish as well. This is not to suggest that anyone who opposes Israeli policies is anti-Jewish. Again, there are many committed Jews who despair about certain Israeli decisions and actions. But it is true that, in some cases, being anti-Israel can slip over into being anti-Jewish. The question was: did this apply to Corbyn? He was definitely anti-Zionist. When Zionism arose, it meant "the establishment of a Jewish homeland". After 1948, it simply meant "the maintenance of a Jewish homeland", and without any reference to what sort of policies or borders. To be anti-Zionist, therefore, means denying Jews the right that most other people enjoyed and singling Jews out as not deserving a homeland of their own. That is perilously close to being anti-Jewish. In addition, Corbyn had made a number of references against Jews, such as saying, effectively, that British Jews did not understand irony. He also defended a mural in East London that was a grotesque portrayal of rich Jewish financiers playing a Monopoly-style board game, resting on the backs of naked downtrodden workers. It was a picture which could have come straight from Goebbels' *Der Stürmer*. It seemed uncomfortably clear that, for whatever reason, Corbyn did not like Jews and did not hide his dislike of Jews.

It was often said that antisemitism was "weaponised" against Corbyn by his political opponents. In reality, it was a massive own goal. When all these revelations came out, the Jewish community became very concerned and approached him to clarify his opinions. Time and time again, he obfuscated or denied there was any issue. He repeatedly refused to apologise for past statements or actions that even gave the impression of being anti-Jewish. It would have been so easy for him to say:

"Look, in the past I have done or said things that could be read the wrong way. I do regret them and let me apologise for those mistakes. As for Israel, there are many of its polices I dislike, but I fully accept its right to exist and I acknowledge that the Jewish people have as much right to a national home as any other people." Even if he did not mean it, it would have been politically savvy to say it! Instead, he took the line that he had a long track record of being anti-racist and therefore could not be anti-Jewish. The feeling began to develop that – whether out of ignorance or wilfulness – he could not see that the one was a cover for the other. He may have been genuinely anti-racist, but he had a blind spot when it came to Israel and the Jews.

The problem was not just with Corbyn himself, but the knock-on effect of his stance. Whatever denials he was making in public, an increasingly large group within Labour seemed to be getting the message that both Israel and Jews were now legitimate targets. Jewish Labour MPs were abused and attempts made to deselect them by their local constituencies. Jewish Labour councillors faced similar barracking from their own party. The term "Zio" (short for Zionist) was hissed at them during internal party meetings. If a Jewish Labour councillor was accused of being "Zio" when discussing local road repairs or rubbish collection, what was this other than antisemitism? Jewish members of the Labour Party no longer felt safe, and one MP even had to have a police guard when attending the Labour Party annual conference. Nobody accused Corbyn of deliberately initiating such a poisonous atmosphere, but it was clear that many elements within the party felt emboldened by his leadership, and he either could not see it or was unable to control it. Alternatively, he did not wish to intervene. Whichever one was true, all were bad news.

I was becoming very discomforted for two reasons. First, it seemed to me that political life was entering a dangerous new phase. There had always been anti-Jewish organisations in

Britain, such as the British National Party or English Defence League, but they had been limited to fringe parties or street yobs. Now, for the first time, a mainstream political party was being infused with the anti-Jewish virus. Astonishingly, it was Labour, which had long been the champion of vulnerable groups in society. Never before had this happened, whether under the leadership of the left, such as Michael Foot, or the right, during Tony Blair's term of office. Second, as someone who felt very much at home in Britain and who always expected to end his days here, I became reminded that I was also the child of someone who had fled her homeland. Might history be about to repeat itself again? It had seemed unthinkable to German Jews in 1932, yet within a few years many were refugees abroad. I did not envisage concentration camps in the UK, but I did foresee life becoming unpleasant enough to want to leave.

I was sure that if I was feeling uneasy about the situation, then so were members of my synagogue. At the *Rosh Hashannah* (Jewish New Year) service in September 2018, one of the times when there is one of the largest attendances of the year, I gave a sermon about Corbyn and his impact, expressed my fears and suggested different ways of responding. For the first time ever in my forty years, it was followed by a standing ovation. It is not Jewish tradition to clap a sermon, let alone stand to do so. It was clear that I had touched a nerve and was articulating the concerns of others. Meanwhile British politics was in turbulence over Brexit, leading to the downfall of Theresa May and Parliament in gridlock over how to proceed. Boris Johnson took over as Prime Minister and subsequently called an election in December 2019. In the previous election, two years earlier, Labour had been narrowly defeated and there was a possibility that this time it could win and Corbyn lead the country.

There has always been an unwritten rule that clergy should not engage in party politics. We may deal with political issues – be it homelessness, the environment or nuclear war – but not use the pulpit to takes sides in an election. I had always observed that, including in the 2017 election when Corbyn led the Labour Party, but where the issue of his antisemitism was still unclear and open to debate. Now the question marks had turned into exclamation marks. I felt the new situation demanded a new response and it was time to cross that red line. I therefore sent an email to every member of the community, who were scattered over several counties, suggesting they should vote for whichever party is most likely to defeat Labour in whatever constituency they are in, even if they would never normally vote for that party. I made it clear that this was not a vote against Labour per se, but against Corbyn-led Labour. I felt sufficiently strongly about the issue that I wanted to not limit it to my area but to galvanise others as much as possible, both within and without the Jewish community. I therefore released the email to the *Jewish Chronicle*, which devoted the whole of its front page to it that week, and I also wrote substantive articles for *The Times* and the *Daily Mail*. It was a call not just to Jews, but to all people of goodwill who opposed prejudice and discrimination to vote against Corbyn. It resulted in numerous television and radio interviews, as well as headlines in other papers such as "Rabbi tells flock 'keep Corby out'" (*The Sun*), "Rabbi urges tactical votes against Labour" (*Daily Express*) and "Rabbi issues stark warning" (*Australian Jewish News*). Corbynistas were not pleased and I was contacted by the Police Commissioner and offered police protection, along with an officer standing outside my home. I declined. I might have been worried about right-wing threats, but took the attitude (or gamble?) that the left-wing would use rhetoric and invective rather than bottles and knives.

The response was fascinating. Within my own community, there was near unanimous support, with only four people expressing reservations and one person very disturbed by it. Amongst my rabbinic colleagues there was great opposition. Some disagreed about the level of threat Corbyn presented, while others agreed with my analysis but still felt it was wrong for a rabbi to speak out in this way. I also know there were those who were angry because they now felt pressurised by their own congregants to take a view either way. Only one other rabbi, Yuval Keren of Southgate Progressive Synagogue, emailed his members to the same effect. The wider Jewish community, however, largely welcomed the move and saw it as giving rabbinic leadership that had been conspicuously absent. It led the Chief Rabbi to "come out" two weeks later, and although he did not suggest how people should vote, he did condemn Corbyn's antisemitism.

As is well known, Corbyn not only lost the election but led Labour to its worst ever electoral defeat since the 1930s. There were many factors behind this, including an extremely left-wing manifesto that alienated many voters and a confused approach to Brexit that put off others. There is no doubt, though, that his antisemitism played a factor in two ways. First, it offended many people's sense of natural justice and fair play; it was not the British way of doing things. Second, one of the reasons Corbyn had attracted such support initially was the aura of integrity around him: the man who had been in the political wilderness for so long because of his principled stand on various issues. His antisemitic comments in earlier years, and his refusal later to acknowledge them or apologise, dented that image considerably. Now people began to realise why he had been in the wilderness for so long. As one person told me: "If he can have a blind spot about antisemitism, what others blind spots does he have?" Chants of "Oooh Jeremy Corbyn" began to turn into sighs of "Oh, Corbyn". If I played a small part in his downfall, I consider that an achievement.

* * *

The above is a short reflection of four very diverse causes which

I have espoused, encompassing pastoral, educational and political issues, and with each one bringing a mix of vilification and praise. For me, though, none of them was controversial; instead they were simply a matter of common sense and, in the case of mixed-faith couples and assisted dying, compassion. Still, it is always hard to know how others perceive one, and I had a glimpse recently when the BBC asked me to take part in Radio 4's *The Moral Maze*. I had appeared on it before, but was surprised to be invited this time, as the subject was religious authority, which is not something I consider to be my area of expertise. When I asked why they wanted me on the programme, the producer charmingly said, "Because you are known as the disobedient rabbi." I am still working out whether that is positive or not.

Either way, it does raise a wider issue that applies to virtually all rabbis, vicars and priests. To what extent can you plough your own furrow before getting into trouble and be hauled in to see someone more senior. I have been very fortunate in being part of a movement, Reform Judaism, that has a distinctive identity but allows great flexibility within it. Each congregation is part of it, yet autonomous within it. There is an Assembly of Reform Rabbis, which decides overall policy, but allows considerable individual freedom, providing one does not stray too far away from it. It is a very generous attitude that allows Reform rabbis to breathe more freely than some others can. It has also enabled the movement to adapt, develop and stay fresh, rather than become ossified. So many religious movements which start off as reformist end up becoming new orthodoxies, leading to groups breaking away and setting up independently. I have also been lucky in having a very tolerant community, with whom there has been an unwritten deal: do your congregational work well, especially the pastoral side, and we will not object to you pursuing your own causes, even if we do not approve of them all. I am very aware that other colleagues have had difficult relations with their Council if they step out of line, even resulting in dismissal. It reinforces my theory of rabbinic life that I mentioned earlier: if your congregants feel loved and valued, then you can be forgiven for what they would not forgive if they did not like you.

Chapter 11

Going Forward

Are you still here?

I sometimes wonder if the Methodists have got it right. They have the tradition that their ministers only stay in one pulpit for seven years and then move to a new one. There is the obvious advantage that they do not become complacent in one position, while they bring new energy and perspective to each successive community. It means, too, that congregants experience a variety of different religious voices. It also occurs to me that it enables the minister to recycle his sermons every seven years to a new congregation that had not heard them before (assuming they went down reasonably well when first delivered). Speaking as someone who has just completed his fortieth year in the same place, I fully recognise that staying put for so long carries the danger of losing creativity and sinking into a rut. As my current chair expressed it so elegantly: "Forty years – you don't get that for murder!" I have tried to avoid this downside by constantly setting new tasks for myself within the synagogue, as well as being involved in national causes (as covered in the previous chapter). However, there is also the big advantage that you become the family rabbi and span the generations. I am doing the baby blessing of parents, whose own baby blessing I did, whose parents I married and whose grandparents I buried. I have shared their joys and their sadnesses, as well as some of the messy bits in between. To my mind, the richness of that experience vastly outweighs the pitfalls.

In this vein, I have often been puzzled by the medical consultants I have had to see at various points in my life. They spent time with me over a period of months, got involved in my life, gave me good advice and resolved my problem. But then signed me off, moved on to their next patient and never saw me again. I understand that is the nature of their job, but to me that sort of short contact would be very frustrating, compared to seeing a patient over several decades, as do family GPs. Of course, this pattern is not for everyone, so I am not advocating it as the ideal way, just as one of many rabbinic options that, given the right circumstances, can work well. Just for the record, in case anyone thinks Maidenhead has suffered too much from my longevity, the community has flourished, whether in terms of membership (from some 75 families when I came to the 850 now) or range of activities. The growth in size means we have had to move once and renovate on site twice, so we are now effectively in our fourth building.

As I mentioned much earlier, I am often asked if my sons – I have four – have followed in my footsteps. Some people ask out of curiosity, as much to know what they are doing if they have not pursued rabbinic studies. Some ask out of assumption, reckoning that it would be obvious that such intense exposure to Jewish life would result in similar piety. Others ask out of validation, thinking that it is the sign of a successful rabbi that his children copy his example (and, by inference, a black mark against him if they do not). I suspect vicars go through the same interrogation. Depending on who asks me, and how, I either say no, they have chosen different paths; or I point out that my father was not a rabbi, and I did not follow his footsteps, so why should I expect my children to follow mine? But for those with a sense of humour, I say: "yes, two did – one went into advertising and the other is an actor." In reality, it is a semi-serious remark, for advertising Jewish life and pushing communal involvement is the backbone of my work, while anyone who wants to make a half-decent impression in the pulpit has to be able to inject some drama, humour, pathos and even righteous anger in their sermons.

Dare and dare and dare again

Given that none of us knows what lies around the corner, one of the things that can help us deal best with whatever looms ahead is a really good motto. Short, simple, pithy, but part of the personal armour that can gives us strength to do the right thing, or that can anchor us in our core values. The earliest book of rabbinic literature, the Mishnah, completed in the second century, has quite a few to offer. There is Hillel saying: "If I am not for myself, who is for me? [in other words, we have to stick up for our own rights] But if I am only for myself, what am I? [being self-obsessed is equally wrong] And if not now, when?" [Theological debate is fine, but there is a time to stop theorising and start acting.]

A contemporary of his was Shammai, who summed up his life's teachings as: "Say little, do much, and welcome everyone cheerfully". As a religious paraphrase, it is superb: it rolls off the tongue easily, but also covers a wide range of situations. Whereas Hillel and Shammai are well known in Jewish circles for their many other achievements, another rabbi from that period – who might otherwise have disappeared from popular memory – has become famous because his personal motto has been adopted as a modern slogan by Jews campaigning for various causes. He was Rabbi Tarphon, who declared: "It is not your duty to complete the work, but neither are you free to desist from it." It has inspired those, for instance, battling against the odds to save millions threatened by famine, or to inoculate children against malaria, or to rescue animals caught up in an oil slick. The overall task may be more than you can manage, but at least make your contribution to it.

There are even earlier examples of sacred one-liners that are more helpful than long lists of commandments when battling to get through the day. The five words of Leviticus – "Love your neighbour as yourself" – are unbeatable as a general guide to life. Even more succinct is the cry of Moses to Pharaoh: "Let my people go". Whereas some biblical phrases have had limited usage, that one has echoed across the centuries and has been heard in recent decades by figures such as Martin Luther King and Nelson Mandela in their respective struggles.

Among the modern sayings that have inspired me personally is one by Rabbi Harold Reinhart who said: "It is not what people want that counts, it is what they ought to want". I am also guided by Mendel of Kotzk: "Take care of your own soul and another person's body… but not of your own body and another person's soul." That is very powerful. The words of two of my own teachers have also left a deep impression on me. One was Louis Jacobs who used to say in class: "Better to be probably right than definitely wrong," while Lionel Blue held that "Religious cooking is generous cooking" reminding of the importance of hospitality and always having an extra place at the table. However, the one that I instinctively adopted for myself was after seeing George Bernard Shaw's play *Joan of Arc* as a teenager. It is from a scene when she is surrounded by men telling her to go home and forget about her vision, to which she responded: "I will dare and dare and dare again". That line has stayed with me ever since then. It has given me the impetus to speak out on so many issues upon which it would have been easier to keep quiet, and to persevere when others then tried to silence me.

Another secret weapon I have had is a strong fantasy life from an early age. I think it started when I was around 11 years old, but it has remained with me ever since and is still hyperactive. It is based on never being satisfied with who I am, having a strong vision of who I would like to be, and has led me to constantly try to bridge the gap. It may sound like a recipe for permanent discontent, but instead it has been a constant spur to improve myself. Sometimes I have succeeded and have been really pleased at the changes, other times I have fallen short of my self-expectations and am still striving to reach them. Either way, though, I would have definitely been less spirited without those images of my better self.

What is it really like being a minister of religion? There are moments of *The Vicar of Dibley*, dealing with dotty parishioners, but much more *Rev.*, wading through social dilemmas and individual crises. It is certainly an overtime job, and I have rarely been to bed the same day that I got up. Yet it is also a lot of fun and joy. Far from being locked in a pious ivory tower, a minister is probably one of the most challenging and all-encompassing jobs a person can have.

Author Biography

Rabbi, writer and broadcaster, Jonathan Romain is minister of Maidenhead Synagogue in Berkshire. He writes for *The Times* and *The Jewish Chronicle* and is often heard on the BBC, while *The Naked* Rabbi is his nineteenth book. In 2004, he received the MBE for his pioneering work nationally in helping mixed-faith couples. He is chaplain to the Jewish Police Association, President of the Accord Coalition (which campaigns for inclusive education) and chair of IFDiD (Inter Faith leaders for Dignity in Dying). For several years he was a judge for both *The Times* Preacher of the Year Award and the BBC's Frank Gillard Awards, and was a member of the BBC's Standing Conference on Religion and Belief. He is a past Chairman of the Assembly of Rabbis UK and is on the Council of St George's House, Windsor Castle.

CHRISTIAN ALTERNATIVE
BOOKS

THE NEW OPEN SPACES

Throughout the two thousand years of Christian tradition there have been, and still are, groups and individuals that exist in the margins and upon the edge of faith. But in Christianity's contrapuntal history it has often been these outcasts and pioneers that have forged contemporary orthodoxy out of former radicalism as belief evolves to engage with and encompass the ever-changing social and scientific realities. Real faith lies not in the comfortable certainties of the Orthodox, but somewhere in a half-glimpsed hinterland on the dirt track to Emmaus, where the Death of God meets the Resurrection, where the supernatural Christ meets the historical Jesus, and where the revolution liberates both the oppressed and the oppressors.

Welcome to Christian Alternative... a space at the edge where the light shines through.
If you have enjoyed this book, why not tell other readers by posting a review on your preferred book site.
Recent bestsellers from Christian Alternative are:

Bread Not Stones

The Autobiography of An Eventful Life
Una Kroll
The spiritual autobiography of a truly remarkable woman and a history of the struggle for ordination in the Church of England.
Paperback: 978-1-78279-804-0 ebook: 978-1-78279-805-7

The Quaker Way
A Rediscovery
Rex Ambler
Although fairly well known, Quakerism is not well understood.
The purpose of this book is to explain how Quakerism works as
a spiritual practice.
Paperback: 978-1-78099-657-8 ebook: 978-1-78099-658-5

Blue Sky God
The Evolution of Science and Christianity
Don MacGregor
Quantum consciousness, morphic fields and blue-sky
thinking about God and Jesus the Christ.
Paperback: 978-1-84694-937-1 ebook: 978-1-84694-938-8

Celtic Wheel of the Year
Tess Ward
An original and inspiring selection of prayers combining
Christian and Celtic Pagan traditions, and interweaving their
calendars into a single pattern of prayer for every morning
and night of the year.
Paperback: 978-1-90504-795-6

Christian Atheist
Belonging without Believing
Brian Mountford
Christian Atheists don't believe in God but miss him: especially
the transcendent beauty of his music, language, ethics, and
community.
Paperback: 978-1-84694-439-0 ebook: 978-1-84694-929-6

Compassion Or Apocalypse?
A Comprehensible Guide to the Thought of René Girard
James Warren
How René Girard changes the way we think about God and the
Bible, and its relevance for our apocalypse-threatened world.
Paperback: 978-1-78279-073-0 ebook: 978-1-78279-072-3

Diary Of A Gay Priest
The Tightrope Walker
Rev. Dr. Malcolm Johnson
Full of anecdotes and amusing stories, but the Church is still a
dangerous place for a gay priest.
Paperback: 978-1-78279-002-0 ebook: 978-1-78099-999-9

Do You Need God?
Exploring Different Paths to Spirituality Even For Atheists
Rory J.Q. Barnes
An unbiased guide to the building blocks of spiritual belief.
Paperback: 978-1-78279-380-9 ebook: 978-1-78279-379-3

Readers of ebooks can buy or view any of these bestsellers by
clicking on the live link in the title. Most titles are published
in paperback and as an ebook. Paperbacks are available in
traditional bookshops. Both print and ebook formats are
available online.

Find more titles and sign up to our readers' newsletter at
http://www.johnhuntpublishing.com/christianity
Follow us on Facebook at
https://www.facebook.com/ChristianAlternative

What people are saying about

the bottom

In this startlingly fresh and challenging book, Charles (Chaz) Lattimore Howard engages in a very personal and deeply embodied form of theology that moves from abstraction to flesh-and-blood human experience. As he journeys "downward" to build real relationships with sisters and brothers living on the streets, he invites the reader on that mysterious journey to meet those on the margins, where we discover harsh truths about social injustice and dehumanization. But we also discover our truest selves—and ultimately come to know more intimately the passionate love of God.

Sister Mary Scullion RSM, Co-Founder and Executive Director of Project HOME and internationally recognized world leader in addressing homelessness

The Bottom: A Theopoetic of the Streets is a profoundly moving work that liberates our preconceived notions of theology, literature, and poetry. Chaz speaks to our collective conscience in the necessity and beauty of reorienting our vision; from the top to the bottom. With each successive chapter, one is led to seeing the glory of God in the fullness of one another. Thus, it may be organized as a book when, in fact, it is a living prayer.

The Rt. Rev. Daniel G. P. Gutiérrez, XVI Bishop, Episcopal Diocese of Pennsylvania

This book is proof of the gifted writer Nnedi Okorafor's wisdom and warning: "Words are powerful when chosen well and hurled with precision." Dr. Howard's hurled poetic prose is a timely testimony that challenges, enlightens, and surprises in deep ways. There is terrible and beautiful truth here, excavated by daring explorative living and thinking. If you let yourself receive what it offers, your understandings of God, Self, and Other will be transformed forever.

Kirk Byron Jones, Professor Emeritus, Andover Newton Theological School, and author of *Soul Talk: How to Have the Most Important Conversation of All*

I once heard a preacher say that we should be careful as we climb the ladder of success and upward mobility, lest on our way up we pass Jesus on his way down. The entire story of Jesus is about a God who leaves the comfort of heaven to join the suffering here on earth, a God who hears the cries of the oppressed. We have a Savior who comes to us as a brown-skinned Palestinian Jewish refugee in the middle of a genocide and who dies a victim of state-sanctioned execution, naked, tortured, humiliated, hanging on the empire's cross. Chaz Howard has penned a smooth book that flows like blues, and jazz, and the freedom songs. It's a book that moved me in the space beyond words and pixels, in the depths of my soul. Read it, and read it again, and pass it around. Here is the Gospel of Chaz, inviting us to descend into holiness.

Shane Claiborne, author, speaker, activist, and Co-Founder of Red Letter Christians

To know Chaz is to know love. Far deeper than sentimentality, this is the kind of love that is akin to "soul force" that became the hallmark of Gandhi and Martin Luther King Jr.'s movements. It is transformative, inclusive—and revolutionary. As a minister, Chaz shared this presence through his uncommon sermons. As the youngest chaplain in the history of UPenn, students came to know him for his deep listening. And now, as an author, we get to see the world through his remarkable lens of radical love and holy play. What a joy!

Nipun Mehta, Founder of ServiceSpace.org, an incubator of projects that works at the intersection of volunteerism, technology, and the gift-economy